WISEGUYS SAY
THE DARNDEST
THINGS

THE QUOTABLE MAFIA

WISEGUYS SAY THE DARNDEST THINGS
THE QUOTABLE MAFIA

JERRY CAPECI

ALPHA

A member of Penguin Group (USA) Inc.

International Standard Book Number: 1-59257-083-6
Library of Congress Catalog Card Number: 2004100482

06   05   04   8   7   6   5   4   3   2   1

Interpretation of the printing code: The rightmost number of the first series of numbers is the year of the book's printing; the rightmost number of the second series of numbers is the number of the book's printing. For example, a printing code of 04-1 shows that the first printing occurred in 2004.

Printed in the United States of America

Note: This publication contains the opinions and ideas of its author. It is intended to provide helpful and informative material on the subject matter covered. It is sold with the understanding that the author and publisher are not engaged in rendering professional services in the book. If the reader requires personal assistance or advice, a competent professional should be consulted.

The author and publisher specifically disclaim any responsibility for any liability, loss, or risk, personal or otherwise, which is incurred as a consequence, directly or indirectly, of the use and application of any of the contents of this book.

Trademarks: All terms mentioned in this book that are known to be or are suspected of being trademarks or service marks have been appropriately capitalized. Alpha Books and Penguin Group (USA) Inc. cannot attest to the accuracy of this information. Use of a term in this book should not be regarded as affecting the validity of any trademark or service mark.

Most Alpha books are available at special quantity discounts for bulk purchases for sales promotions, premiums, fund-raising, or educational use. Special books, or book excerpts, can also be created to fit specific needs.

For details, write: Special Markets, Alpha Books, 375 Hudson Street, New York, NY 10014.

For Haley Elizabeth Capeci, a very quotable two-year-old who recently uttered a most memorable line,
"I love you Grandpaw."

Contents

Quotes, Quips, and Anecdotes About ...

Introduction

"Listen carefully to me. You'll never see another guy like me if you live to be 5,000."

—John Gotti, January 29, 1998.

Whether John Gotti was speaking to his relatives, as he did above, or the law, the media, or his crime family, the late Dapper Don had an uncanny way with words. From the day he burst on the scene during the 1985 Christmas season, until his death from cancer in 2002, the former truck hijacker from Queens could deliver a line with the best of them.

"I'm the boss of my family—my wife and kids at home," he declared at his first public appearance after he orchestrated the spectacular assassination of his boss, when reporters asked if he now headed the Gambino family. Like a skilled politician on the stump, Gotti pushed his way into the courthouse, always smiling broadly for the cameras. Until he and a woman reporter arrived together at the courtroom door. "I was brought up to hold the door open for ladies," he smiled, ushering her in with a flourish.

Gotti waxed poetic, often tossing in references to literary works or Sunday newspaper comic strips: "I'm ready for Freddy," he said, using the name of the undertaker in the old *Smilin' Jack* strip when he reported to prison to await trial in 1986. "Fear is a stronger emotion than love, read Machiavelli," he quipped more than once.

"I ain't no Dagwood," he chortled after a smiling Lisa Gastineau told him he could call her Blondie, as her friends had done since she was a little girl.

For all his wit, charm, pizzazz, and ego, however, Gotti was only one man, with one perspective. In *Wiseguys Say the Darndest Things: The Quotable Mafia*, you get words from scores of other wiseguys, and people who knew, loved, hated, or respected them, to give you a fuller picture of the entire Mafia landscape.

During Gotti's heyday, for example, he was caught on tape telling a crew member to deliver a message to a rival mob associate who was infringing on the Dapper Don's territory: "You tell him, I, me, John Gotti will sever his mother fucking head." The theory behind Gotti's actions were stated quite succinctly by Colombo soldier Salvatore Profaci in another tape-recorded conversation about a garbage collecting dispute between the Genovese and Philadelphia crime families: "Good fellows don't sue good fellows, good fellows kill good fellows."

"This life is a losing proposition. No matter what we do we can't win," Gambino associate Dominick Montiglio complained one day.

"Maybe so," said crime buddy Henry Borelli, "but it beats working."

These are real words uttered by real people. There are no quotes from Don Corleone or Tony Soprano in this book. We do, however, have some words of wisdom about murder and mob mayhem from New Jersey gangsters who fancy themselves as the models for *The Sopranos*, the hit HBO television series about a fictional crime family from the Garden State.

Like Gotti's and Profaci's utterances, the remarks of the real-life mobsters about HBO's reel-life gangsters come from FBI tape recordings. In March 1999, New Jersey wiseguys Joseph "Tin Ear" Sclafani and Anthony Rotondo were driving to a mob sit-down with rival gangsters when the television show came up.

"Hey, what's this fucking thing, *Sopranos*. What the fuck are they … Is that supposed to be us?" exclaimed Sclafani.

"You're in there, they mentioned your name in there," said Rotondo.

"Yeah? What did they say?" Sclafani asked.

Back and forth they went, mentioning similarities between their own mob crew and crime family landmarks with those portrayed on the hit show until Rotondo capped the discussion with the observation: "What characters. Great acting."

Introduction

Like most Americans, the gangsters in *Wiseguys Say the Darndest Things* speak about their work and pleasure; their everyday likes and dislikes. They discuss killing and a variety of chores that go with the life they chose. But they also talk about their childhood, their wives and girlfriends, and a litany of other things, including problems they face, day in and day out.

In early 2003, Bonanno capo Frank "Curly" Lino had a big problem and solved it the way lots of wiseguys do when they are charged with murder. He cooperated. In the summer of 1999, however, Lino had a different problem when Manhattan Federal Judge Denny Chin told him to report to prison on September 10 to begin serving 57 months for stock fraud. Lino had pleaded guilty and knew what the sentence would be, but he had a problem with the timing. "Uh, Your Honor, I, uh, have tickets to uh, a baseball game that night ... Could you, uh ...." he stammered, adding that it was a Yankees–Red Sox game. "September 14 then," said Chin. "I'm a Yankee fan, too."

In this book you'll read what mobsters say about their lawyers, celebrities, and why it's dangerous to be driving on Monday and Thursday mornings. You'll read what wiseguys from all over the country have to say about how to avoid bugs and wiretaps, the right and wrong ways to kill a guy, and how to recover from emotional stress. And honor, loyalty, the death penalty, the food they like, and the women they love.

Sprinkled throughout the book are snippets of remarkable conversations. Many of them are exchanges between Genovese family soldiers Federico "Fritzy" Giovanelli and Frank "Frankie California" Condo in which the men chatter like two old hens about recipes, vitamins, diet, getting old, Florida vacations, rigged card games, their girlfriends and wives, Mussolini, the 10 O'clock News, and so much more. "It's *Seinfeld* meets *The Sopranos:* A series about nuttin'," said The Smoking Gun website, which first published the profane but funny and whimsical conversations that were taped by the FBI as part of a racketeering investigation in late 1985 and early 1986.

Interestingly, the values of "wiseguys"—and for purposes of this book we use the term to refer to gangsters of all ethnic persuasions—are often similar and transcend the position or rank they have, the area of the country where they operate, or the era in which they lived and died—and many died violently at the hands of former friends.

Culled from thousands of tape recordings, court testimony, other documents, books, and interviews by the author, the book features wiseguys discussing television, the movies, and just about everything else that they, and normal people, talk about in their daily routine. We've got the inside dope about loansharking, gambling, extortion, the law, and the media from Al Capone of Chicago, Dutch Schultz of New York, Santo Trafficante of Tampa, Whitey Bulger of Boston, and many more.

As this book went to press, longtime Bonanno associate Murray Kufeld was in McKean Federal Prison in Virginia on a drug rap. In the summer of 1999, however, Kufeld was not charged with any crimes and in a feisty mood as he fielded questions from assistant U.S. attorney Jim Walden. Kufeld was a reluctant witness, one the federal prosecutor was using to try to establish that Kufeld's longtime buddy, Anthony Spero, was a Bonanno consigliere who ran a mob social club that was a haven for gangsters, and deserved to be jailed as he awaited trial for murder.

Walden: The pet shop you're referring to is owned by Sal Spero, Mr. Spero's brother, right?

Kufeld: Yes.

Walden: That's in fact, a meeting place for members and associates of the Bonannos.

Kufeld: That's a meeting place for pigeon flyers.

Walden: What pigeon flyers meet at the pet shop that you referred to as a social club?

Kufeld: Well, there's Sally; there's Billy; there's Victor; there's Victor's son Frank; there's Charlie.

Introduction

Walden: Do you have last names for us?

Kufeld: Not really.

Walden: You don't know the last names of any of these people?

Kufeld: No.

Walden: Well, do you know anyone's last name?

Kufeld: I think I just heard one, Billy Something-or-Other.

Walden: What about a man named Petey Boxcars?

Kufeld: I've seen him.

Walden: Who's his father?

Kufeld: His father was Patty Boxcars.

A few minutes later, Walden pressed for the names of the pigeon people again, saying he was going to write them down.

Kufeld: There's Charlie, there's Billy; there's Victor; there's Frankie; there's Skippy and various other people that fly pigeons.

Walden: What's Victor's last name?

Kufeld: I can't tell you. I don't know his last name.

Walden: What is Frank's name?

Kufeld: Frank is Victor's son. I don't know their last name.

Walden: Understood. What's Skippy's real first name?

Kufeld: Really don't know him by anything other than Skippy.

Walden: And this is a complete list of people that you know.

Kufeld: No. There are various other people that go there that I don't know.

Much of the material in this book is hilarious. All of it, we believe, is entertaining and informative. Between murder plots and stock scams, and when they're not tied up in court battles, wiseguys also enjoy a good read, especially when it's about them.

Genovese mobster Salvatore "Sammy Meatballs" Aparo expressed respect for *New York Times* reporters. "The *Times*, they got good people working for them," he said.

Gotti and another Sammy quoted extensively in this book—Salvatore "Sammy Bull" Gravano—were perusing a new book in their Little Italy social club one day when Gotti noticed that the author had wrongly reported that his parents had emigrated from Italy in steerage. Gotti exploded, "These fucking bums that write books, they're worse than us."

Finally, a Mafia book even John Gotti would have enjoyed.

Jerry Capeci
New York City
November 9, 2003

Acknowledgments

Many quotes in this book stem from my original reporting. Many more, however, were previously reported by other authors, and newspaper, radio, television, and cyberspace reporters—much too many to even think of naming them. Without their work, this book would never have happened.

I do acknowledge, however, two people very close to me—my daughter Jenna and my wife Barbara—whose help was invaluable in finding, gathering, and organizing much of the material in this book. For this, and many other things, I am eternally grateful to them.

At Alpha books, I thank publisher Marie Butler-Knight and the other members of the Alpha family who helped put together the book you have in your hand—Gary Goldstein, Dawn Werk, Paul Dinas, Christy Wagner, and Billy Fields.

A special thank you to development editor Jennifer Moore for her guidance, patience, stick-to-it attitude, creativity, and overall professionalism.

Bugs

"Don't let your tongue be your worst enemy."

> —John "Sonny" Franzese advising
> his son Michael never to say any-
> thing of consequence on the tele-
> phone or in an enclosed room.

"This is the safest territory in the world for a big meet.
We got three towns just outside Chicago with the
police chiefs in our pocket. We got this territory locked
up."

> —Chicago outfit boss Sam
> "Momo" Giancana telling Buffalo
> boss Stefano Magaddino that the
> 1957 Mafia conclave would never
> have been rousted if it were held in
> the Windy City area instead of at
> Apalachin, New York.

"I know one place that's absolutely not bugged: the
Holiday Inn on I-95. That's where the niggers stay and
they don't bug them."

> —Santo Trafficante on where he
> would go to so he could talk to Jimmy
> Hoffa before Hoffa left for prison.

"Ain't nothing going to happen to him ... yet."

> —Salvatore "Wayne" Grande on whether Thomas DelGiorno was in danger of being whacked, tape-recorded words that convinced DelGiorno to cooperate when the feds played the tape for him.

"You know when I hear something good about a guy, I'll probably be in jail, because I get caught on tape bragging about it."

> —John Gotti.

"From now on, I'm telling you that if a guy just so mentions 'La,' I'm gonna strangle the cocksucker. You know what I mean? He don't have to say 'Cosa Nostra,' just 'La' and he goes. I heard nine months of tapes of my life. I was actually sick, and I don't wanna get sick. Not sick for me, sick for 'this thing of ours,' sick for how naive we were five years ago. I'm sick that we were so fucking naive. Me, number one!"

> —John Gotti.

"Hey, you gotta do me a favor. Don't make nobody talk. This is how we get in trouble, we talk."

> —John Gotti stating the obvious on an FBI bug.

Bugs

"These guys didn't talk with footnotes. ... None of it is all that clear or all that direct. Lots of it is impenetrable. Lazy listeners could have easily missed it."

—Michael "Iron Mike" DeFeo, deputy director of the Justice Department's Organized Crime Strike Force in 1978, describing wiretaps.

"We gotta, we got to whisper."

—John Gotti telling Salvatore "Sammy Bull" Gravano how to avoid getting overheard on a bug.

"You know if you talk lower than that [radio] and there's a bug in the joint they won't get the conversation. If you talk higher than that they will."

—Joseph "Bayonne Joe" Zicarelli saying pretty much the same thing to Simone "Sam the Plumber" DeCavalcante 30 years earlier.

"... you feel like you're being raped with those fucking tapes."

—John Gotti on listening to himself on FBI tapes.

"He was never in my fuckin' house talking. Nothin' to put us in fuckin' jail …. Because you know why, Sammy? You gotta relax in your fuckin' house. The way we're relaxing right here."

> —John Gotti telling Sammy
> Bull Gravano why he never let
> Angelo Ruggiero in his house.

"The FBI agents are listening in."

> —Angelo Ruggiero to his mother
> after they heard noise on the line.

"The danger with the phone, even for wiseguys, is that it's so easy. You talk on it all day long and all night long saying nothing. Your wife orders groceries. You find out the correct time. You call Grandma about dinner Sunday. You begin to forget that it's live. That it can hang you."

> —Henry Hill.

"It's getting so bad that when we make new guys, we ought to make them undress so we know they ain't wired up. You know, have a ceremony in the nude."

> —Genovese acting boss Barney
> Bellomo states the problem and
> offers a solution to John Gotti
> and Sammy Bull Gravano.

"And when the call finally comes you're not going to hear ordinary intelligible sentences of a person ordering a commodity on terms and price and conditions. What you will hear is people talking in codes about shirts and shoes and pants and the old pants and the new pants and the architect and the engineer and the work over there and plants and potatoes and cheese, anything but what they are really talking about, which is heroin and cocaine and kilograms and dollars and cents."

—Assistant U.S. Attorney Robert Stewart, telling jurors a primer on how to interpret gangster talk they would hear on tape at a racketeering trial.

Celebrities

"They helped me become what I am today. And now the FBI says that if I see one of these guys who helped me walking down the street, I'm supposed to go to the other side to avoid them. Well, I'm not going to do that."

> —Frank Sinatra reminiscing with
> Santo Trafficante and Frank
> Ragano about mutual friends
> and mob bosses.

"Listen, Sammy, I don't give a shit about a million people watching you on the Ed Sullivan show. You can't go around breaking your word. Now you listen to me and you hear me right. You get your ass down here and do what you promised to do."

> —Joe Fischetti, Frank Sinatra's
> right-hand man, explaining to
> Sammy Davis Jr. why he shouldn't
> cancel out on an appearance at a
> convention for Jimmy Hoffa.

"I don't want to hear that shit about you can't get plane reservations. Nigger, you get your ass down here even if it means you have to sprout wings to fly."

>—Joe Fischetti in a menacing voice
>to Sammy Davis Jr. Sammy
>honored his commitment and
>sang and danced at the dinner.

"We've got certain ground rules. One of them is no women, no girls. And Frank [Sinatra] will see these guys for thirty minutes. Frank will have a couple of drinks with them, and that's it."

>—Joe Fischetti setting up a
>meeting between Frank Sinatra
>and Santo Trafficante.

"First of all, you tell that goddamn queer we don't lend less than a million dollars. And even if he asked for a million, I wouldn't lend it to that fucking queer faggot."

>—Jimmy Hoffa rejecting Liberace's
>request for a $500,000
>loan from the Teamsters.

"If we ever hit that guy you'll break his jaw. Then he can't sing."

>—Sam Giancana expressing his feelings
>about entertainer Dean Martin.

"That fucking prima donna. You can't call him. I gotta go there and lay the law down to him. 'Hey Dean, this is a must. Sam wants you for ten days!'"

—Johnny Formosa, Chicago Outfit rep in Las Vegas, responding to boss Sam Giancana's request to call Dean Martin for a booking.

"This is a gourmet soup made famous by Al Yeganah, the famous soup Nazi on *Seinfeld*."

—Mob-connected businessman James Chickara dropping names as he lays out a few fraud schemes to mob associate Frank Persico.

"What a jerk. He didn't say anything nice. He froze. Despite all the time John spent with him. He's not a man."

—Gambino capo John "Jackie Nose" D'Amico about Mickey Rourke after the actor ducked television reporters who tried to interview him after he showed up at the racketeering and murder trial of John Gotti.

"This is the best drama going on in America right now. This is the greatest theatre you can possibly see."

> —Actor Anthony Quinn telling reporters why he stopped in to see Salvatore "Sammy Bull" Gravano take the witness stand at the Gotti trial.

"Albert, tomorrow the good guys are going to bring in Clint Eastwood."

> —Federal prosecutor Andy Maloney, to Gotti's lawyer Albert Krieger, after Quinn—who frequently portrayed gangsters in the movies—visited Gotti at his 1992 trial.

Childhood

"Other kids are brought up nice and sent to Harvard and Yale. Me? I was brought up like a mushroom."

—Frank Costello.

"Being tough is learned behavior spawned by necessity. I could hit hard, a 'talent' I carried into adulthood and found out early that someone who was good at fighting usually doesn't have to."

—Eddie Maloney.

"I rode with him, he told me, so it wouldn't look so suspicious because he had a little kid in the truck."

—Former Philadelphia underboss
Philip Leonetti explaining why,
when he was 10 or 11 years old,
his uncle Nicodemo "Little
Nicky" Scarfo, picked him up
right after he had killed someone
and had disposed of the body.

Childhood

"I got into a few minor scrapes, fistfights as a young fellow, and naturally those things go on, and if you stand on your toes and fight back, you soon get that kind of reputation. The man who is thrown out on the street, naturally, that is what happens."

> —Johnny Rosselli, explaining his
> reputation as an enforcer.

"My father believed there was nothing more of value to be learned in school and thought I could benefit from being close to him."

> —Santo Trafficante describing how
> he dropped out of high school and
> began working with his father.

"Nobody had it worse than I had it in life ... I wasn't born with four fucking cents."

> —John Gotti.

"My father had to pay a dollar a week for protection, or else his pushcart would be wrecked .... We were the poorest family on earth. Anyway that's how it seemed to me .... There were three rooms [in our apartment], no hot water, and no bath. The toilet was out in the hall."

> —Joe Valachi.

"My time, all the doors were closed."

—John Gotti, rationalizing
the road he took.

"To me being a wiseguy was better than being president of the United States. It meant power among people who had no power. It meant perks in a working class neighborhood that had no privileges. To be a wiseguy was to own the world. I dreamed about being a wiseguy the way other kids dreamed about being doctors or movie stars or firemen or ballplayers."

—Henry Hill.

"Let me tell you a little story, young fellow. You don't even know what the word name calling is. When you go to school like I went to school with two different color shoes and they call you white trash and mumble all that. You know how many times my mother heard about it. None. None. Zero. That's how many times my mother heard about it."

—John Gotti recalling some childhood experiences to his grandson after hearing that the boy had told his mother that he had been taunted in school by bullies.

"Uncle Peter … takes him to school, punches them in the mouth. That's not being rowdy. That's the man part coming out. You don't know. We went through this when I was a kid. Before you was a kid. When your Uncle Gene had trouble … I went in the school yard and fought them. That's what it's all about. That's what people respected. The next day you see them, they salute you. That's the only course of action. Not the best, the only course of action."

> —John Gotti telling his daughter he would have approved his son Peter, the boy's uncle, retaliating on behalf of his grandson after the bully had called the boy a "little mobster."

"I wouldn't go back and tell my mother. They used to call me names in school. We dusted them off. Broke their heads."

> —John Gotti spells it out for his daughter.

Conversations
with the Law

"I am absolutely 100 percent not a member of organized crime. It's because of that label that I've had all these problems. I'm willing to give the government a pound of flesh if this will be the end of it."

—Michael "The Yuppie Don"
Franzese lying to the government
about his station in life.

"I wish you would have broken that door down. I am going to get the shit bawled out of me for opening it up."

—George Weinberg to the
cops he had just let in.

"Look, if I'm doing anything wrong, why don't you put me in jail. You know every move I make. You know I'm behaving."

—Lucky Luciano to Italian
police who followed him everywhere he went after he was
deported to Italy in 1946.

"What do you want to do? Shoot me? Shoot me, but I'm not going to answer any questions. I'm tired of these charades."

> —Genovese underboss Venero
> "Benny Eggs" Mangano when the
> feds tried to get him to testify
> against Vincent "Chin" Gigante.

"Why don't you go and dig up all the dead ones in the graveyard and ask if I shot them!"

> —Chicago mobster Louis
> Romano's sarcastic retort to a
> Rackets Committee prober's query
> about a large number of people he
> was said to have killed.

"We're all good guys here. You're the good-good guys, and we're the bad-good guys."

> —James "Whitey" Bulger
> to DEA officials.

"You should think about using your friends in law enforcement."

> —FBI agent John Connolly
> to Whitey Bulger.

"You can't survive without friends in law enforcement."

> —Whitey Bulger after the FBI
> offered to eliminate his Mafia rivals.

"I just hope you keep good records, because today or tomorrow if I get charged with a crime, your records will be my alibi."

—Santo Trafficante to the FBI agents following him.

"I am ready to pay for my sins. You got me, put the cuffs on me now and I'll go."

—Luchese family acting boss Steven Crea telling an NYPD detective that he knew the rules of the game and honored them.

A Mafia Parable

Sam "Mad Sam" DeStefano: Mr. Roemer, I ain't no stool pigeon. But here's what I'll do for you. I'll answer your questions by giving you a parable.

FBI Agent William Roemer Jr.: Giving me a parable? I don't understand, Sam.

DeStefano: Here's an example. Coppers came into me a couple weeks ago and said 'You killed them two burglars they found in a trunk.' I said the hell I did, they committed suicide. They said how could they commit suicide, they were both shot in the back of the head. I said they committed suicide when they fucked with Sam DeStefano! That's what I mean by a parable!

"I threw it in an empty lot."

> —Joe Valachi when asked by an
> angry victim what happened to
> $10,000 worth of silk he had stolen
> from his store as the cagey gangster
> wangled a plea bargain to
> "attempted" burglary.

"We weren't allowed to deal junk, we weren't allowed
to kill with bombs, we weren't allowed to violate
another's wives or kids, we weren't allowed to raise our
hands to one another, and they skipped by a few other
rules. They told us that you would be placed with a
captain, and you'll eventually be told all the rules."

> —Salvatore "Sammy Bull" Gravano on
> what he was told when he was inducted
> into the Gambino crime family.

"I knew you were coming tonight. I knew."

> —John Gotti, lying to FBI agents
> as they arrived at his social club
> to arrest him in 1990.

"Now how, sir, could I drive the car and inspect him at
the same time?"

> —Abe "Kid Twist" Reles explaining
> why he didn't know whether a cohort
> had blood on his clothes as they fled
> the scene of a gangland-style slaying.

"Because they were crooks. They thought they were getting a bargain, and I guess greed got them."

> —Philadelphia mobster Nicholas "The Crow" Caramandi on why he was able to con many victims into buying commodities that he really didn't have.

"I got it from a hijacked load. Solve that case."

> —John Gotti to a detective who complimented him on his elegant suit.

"I'm not talking. You stick to your trade and I'll stick to mine."

> —Arnold "The Brain" Rothstein to detectives before he lapsed into a coma after a rubout attempt.

Bosses and Super Bosses

Chicago outfit boss Sam "Momo" Giancana:
I suppose you intend to report this to your boss!

FBI Agent William Roemer Jr.: Who's my boss?

Giancana: J. Edgar Hoover.

Roemer: Yes, I imagine he'll see a copy.

Giancana: Fuck J. Edgar Hoover and your super boss!

Roemer: Who is that?

Giancana: Bobby Kennedy.

Roemer: Might be he'll see a copy, yes.

Giancana: Fuck Bobby Kennedy! And your super, super boss!

Roemer: Who is my super, super boss?

Giancana: John Kennedy!

Roemer: I doubt if the President of the United States is interested in Sam Giancana.

Giancana: Fuck John Kennedy. Listen, Roemer, I know all about the Kennedys, and Phyllis [McGuire] knows more about the Kennedys and one of these days we're going to tell all.

Roemer: What are you talking about?

Giancana: Fuck you. One of these days it'll come out. You wait, you smart asshole, you'll see.

La Cosa Nostra

"No, it's not Mafia. That's the expression the outside uses."

—Joe Valachi.

"Let me tell you how it works. I get money. I don't give you money, you give me money. That's number one."

—Carmine "Junior" Persico giving
the facts of Mafia life to a young
Salvatore "Sammy Bull" Gravano.

"Every week there's a score, $300, or $500 from the dock, so I bring it inside. Then I bring it in to you at Christmas."

—Anthony "Sonny" Ciccone, the
Gambino family's man on the docks
explaining the way he operated to
John Gotti shortly after he took
over as family boss.

"The home is a sanctuary. You can hit people outside the house, but you can't go inside; it's just not considered proper etiquette."

—Joey the Hitman.

"I never did nothing ruthless besides, well, I would kill people. But that's our life."

—Turncoat Philadelphia underboss
Philip Leonetti.

"You know, to me, Cosa Nostra's very sacred. Okay, and my word is better than anything else that I got to offer."

—Colombo capo Salvatore Profaci.

"How I could have put Cosa Nostra ahead of loyalty to my wife and my kids is something I will always have to live with. All my life, growing up, I thought that people who went to school and put their noses to the grindstone were nerds, taking the easy way out. I know now that *I* was the one who took the easy way that I didn't have the balls to stay in school and try. That was the tough road, which I didn't take."

—Sammy Bull Gravano.

"Mario Puzo's book *The Godfather* and the movie they made from it did for the organization what silicon does for tits. They both make their respective subjects stand out. We needed the Godfather like Joey Gallo needed another portion of clams."

—Joey the Hitman.

What Might Have Been

Michael Franzese: Jimmy, if they were going to whack me, would you have told me?

Vincent "Jimmy" Angellino: What would you expect?

Michael: Hell yeah, I'd expect you to tell me!

Jimmy: If they were going to whack me, would you tell me, Michael?

Michael: No. That's sick, isn't it Jimmy? What kind of friends are we? What kind of life is this?

Jimmy: It's our life, Michael. The life we chose. We knew what we were getting into. You especially. You've lived with it from the day you were born.

"No one ever asked me directly if I was in the Mafia. If they had, I don't know what I would have answered, but nobody ever did. It is not a question that you ask somebody."

—Nick Paterno.

"A made man is a full member. Being made means that he has killed somebody, will kill again when told, and because of that has taken the oath that binds him for life to the Mafia. But first, last, and always is the money, because that's what it's all about. Honor, respect, loyalty? That's for the movies."

—Lynda Milito, Mafia wife.

"… nobody gives a fuck about getting in trouble. Listen, that's what *the life* is about, but to get in trouble and not even earn a fucking dollar … that's even worse."

—Genovese soldier Vincent Aparo
badmouthing an especially
incompetent crew member.

"When you get involved with him, you know … you take the good and take the bad. The good is you can run around a lot and have everybody in your circle afraid of you because you got him behind you. The bad is, once in a while you got to do him a favor."

—Thomas "Tommy" DelGiorno,
an earner for Philly mob boss
Nicodemo "Little Nicky" Scarfo.

"The mob guys are always trying to steal from each other. Even when they know somebody's going to wind up in the trunk of a car if they get caught, they still try and steal a few bucks here and there."

—Frank "Lefty" Rosenthal.

"Johnny was the strategist. That was on his [business] card, and that's what he was. Strategy. Protection, Security. How to stay alive."

—Joe Shimon,
an electronics expert.

"Well Willie, anybody who resigns, resigns feet first. Do you understand what that means?"

> —Louis Campagna discussing the
> dangers of trying to resign from the
> Outfit with Willie Bioff.

"Senator, in my business, we don't take notes."

> —Johnny Rosselli in response to a
> question during his testimony
> before the United States Senate.

"People called day or night. Have Louie call Tommy D at the he-knows-where. Tell Louie okay on what he talked to the fat man about. Louie needs to call the guy he was with at the club on Tuesday night. He'll understand. It's important. Tell Louie the three guys in New York say to forget about it and call the skinny guy. He'll know. It's important."

> —Lynda Milito, Mafia wife.

"Someday you could change your mind or your son might run for office. As long as they say things like this, that there is a Mafia, no Sicilian will ever have a chance for a high office."

> —Santo Trafficante telling
> lawyer Frank Ragano that
> the Mafia was a myth.

"There are a lot of people on the street who probably saw us. And today or tomorrow, if something should happen to Manny, those people would never believe that I had anything to do with it."

—Santo Trafficante explaining
why he greeted an informer
like a long-lost friend.

"First of all, if there's no body, the police have a harder time finding out who did it. And number two, some guys do things so bad, you have to punish the families after they're gone."

—Santo Trafficante explaining why
some gangsters disappeared. By
punishing families he meant that
there could be no burial and relatives would be unable to collect life
insurance for seven years.

"But how the hell are you supposed to know who's who? They don't want to tell you. So I started telling people that I met, 'I'm in the Mafia. If you are too, tell me.' That's the way I did it."

—John Veasey expressing
disdain for the formalities
of the organization.

"It's not a toy. I'm not in the mood for the toys or games or kidding. No time. I'm not in the mood for clans. I'm not in the mood for gangs, I'm not in the mood for none a that stuff there. And this is gonna be a Cosa Nostra till I die. Be it an hour from now or be it tonight or a hundred years from now when I'm in jail. It's gonna be a Cosa Nostra. This ain't gonna be a bunch of your friends are gonna be 'friends of ours,' a bunch of Sam's friends are gonna be 'friends of ours.' It's gonna be the way I say it's gonna be, and a Cosa Nostra. A Cosa Nostra."

—John Gotti.

"You know, Frankie, I, I, I don't like you, I love you. I don't like Sammy, I love Sammy. As far as this life, no one knows it better than me. If a guy offends me, I'll break him that's the fuckin' end of it. But not for me. It's this 'thing of ours.' It's gotten to be a circus. I'm not gonna leave a circus when I go to jail, Frankie. I don't wanna be a phony. I ain't gonna talk about a guy behind his back."

—John Gotti, complaining about the poor state of the mob as he lists some of his great attributes to Frank Locascio.

"That's the life I was in. That's the life we're in. That's all—that's all we do over there in that life, kill people, rob people and extort people."

—Turncoat mob associate Dino Basciano.

"Joe, I love you. But I love the *Cosa Nostra* more."

—Simone "Sam the Plumber"
DeCavalcante to Joe Sferra, after he
demoted Sferra for not bringing in
enough business for the men.

"In the end the father of the family is left with the whole mess."

—Sam the Plumber DeCavalcante.

"The Mafia. What is it? It's a brotherhood of evil. It's the code of silence, *omerta.*"

—Nicholas "The Crow" Caramandi.

"This is the biggest thing that the mob has, the people that are around us, and you can have as many people as you want. You could have two guys with you, or ten thousand. It doesn't make any difference, as long as you register 'em with your capo and tell 'em they're with you. You could have a grocery store guy, a politician, a union guy, a judge, a lawyer."

—"The Crow" Caramandi.

"I mean, these were maybe awful things, but they hadda be done."

—"The Crow" Caramandi on
mob hits he'd been part of.

"It's them or us. It's either kill or be killed. Let's get them before they get us."

—Harry Riccobene telling his brother about the mob.

"There's not an industry you could name—entertainment, casinos, construction, the unions—where we don't have something. Wherever there's money, that's where we are. Wherever there's power. You understand? It's a second government. We reach all over, in every major city in the United States. It's nationwide. It's one organization."

—"The Crow" Caramandi, on Cosa Nostra.

"But this thing that the mob does to you when you're young is that they compliment you if you rob, if you kill. The ultimate compliment is when you kill."

—Sammy Bull Gravano.

"That's one of the most important rules in Cosa Nostra. When the boss calls you in, you come in. Or else."

—Sammy Bull Gravano.

"As a wiseguy you can lie, you can cheat, you can steal, you can kill people—*legitimately*. You can do any goddamn thing you want, and nobody can say anything about it. Who wouldn't want to be a wiseguy?'"

—Benjamin "Lefty Guns" Ruggiero.

"Isn't this an honor. I look in the mirror and until this day, I still can't believe it."

—Luchese soldier Rocco Vitulli
on becoming a "made man."

Father Knows Best

Michael "The Yuppie Don" Franzese: Dad. Let me die fighting. Let me die with dignity!

John "Sonny" Franzese: That's not our way, Michael. We will go separately, the way they asked. Whatever happens, happens. It's the right thing, Michael. We are sworn to obey. The oath and the life is more important than any two individuals. I'm going to go. And you must follow. You must!

"This isn't the 1930s. This isn't Al Capone. Those days are gone. We are in a new era. We are not shylocks and pimps and bookmakers. We are businessmen. We have a good thing going here and we can all make a ton of money if we're smart. Murder is not smart. If bodies start showing up everywhere it will bring the police down upon us. We don't want that."

—"The Yuppie Don" Franzese.

"… and he [Joey Aiuppa] wants us to pull his chestnuts out of the fire. I told him to go fuck himself, we can't be responsible if he can't make a go of Cicero. That's a good territory; if he can't make a living in Cicero he must be a real dumb ass."

—Sam Giancana warning Frankie Ferraro that Aiuppa was likely to come running to him for help.

"Ordinarily, before you're a member you'd have to make a hit and I'd have to be with you as your sponsor to verify that you made the hit and report how you handled yourself. But with the reputation you two have, this may not be necessary."

—Boston mobster Peter Limone confiding to Steve "The Rifleman" Flemmi and Frank Salemme that they were going to be asked to join the Mafia.

"I want to enter alive into this organization and leave it dead."

—Carmen Tortora after being inducted into the New England Mafia family in the first induction ceremony that was tape recorded by the FBI.

"You pierce the veil and what you find is a bunch of street thugs with no sophistication. They're really no different than these neighborhood drug gangs … We give them names and put them on charts, but they're no different."

—Louis Pichini, head of the criminal division of the United States Attorney's Office in Philadelphia.

"Isn't it a good thing you could be in the Mafia, right, but nobody knows it? I can do a lot of things for you. If nobody knows."

—Philadelphia capo Joe Sodano, who controlled the family's North Jersey gambling and loan sharking operations, talking about "the life."

"Forty-five miles each way for a thirty-second phone call. These guys are serious about what they do."

—Steve Salvo, an FBI linguistic expert who spoke Sicilian, on watching the moves of a suspected member of a Sicilian Mafia drug network.

"... some of the best guys for this kind of life are guys that are criminals. They're thieves. They stole out of necessity. Other people, come into it, they want to come in with a suit and a tie and thirty pounds over-weight. And then pose. And they never were against the law. They never got kicked in the balls."

—Joe Sodano, again, talking about "the life."

 Frank & Fritzy: No RSVP Necessary

Being a Genovese gangster may have its privileges, but neither Frank nor Fritzy were invited to a so-called friend's ritzy wedding.

Frank: Over there, that guy had a wedding in The Plaza, forget about it ...

Fritzy: Forget about it. You know, ya know why we didn't get a fuckin' invitation?

Frank: Mmm?

Fritzy: 'Cause he didn't want nobody to see who the fuck he invited.

Frank: No. He didn't, eh ...

Frank: [UI] gave ya an invitation.

Fritzy: Who?

Frank: Nah.

Fritzy: Hey, he knew ...

Frank: [UI] everybody.

Fritzy: Pal, he knew how to bother me.

Frank: He gave even The Rubber.

Fritzy: Wha?

Frank: He gave The Rubber an invitation.

Fritzy: Yeah?

Frank: Yeah. You know the guy that rubs me?

Fritzy: Yeah?

Frank: He, he, he got one.

Fritzy: He goes out there, to Brooklyn?

Frank: Yeah, he rubs 'em.

Fritzy: Oh, he does?

Frank: He lives out there.

Fritzy: Wha?

Frank: He lives near there, he knows, he's born around there.

Fritzy: Well, The Rubber is one thing. That don't mean nothin', but I'm ...

Frank: I'm sayin' he gave him one, and ya know he's gonna tell, uh, who is that this guy everything, huh?

Fritzy: Yeah, well, that don't mean nothin'. He gave him one, too. He sent one to him.

Frank: Yeah.

Fritzy: Ya know?

Frank: Uh-huh?

Fritzy: But, uh, I just, I just …

Frank: You didn't get one, huh?

Fritzy: No. No … I happened to be at the fuckin', I happened to be somewhere.

Frank: Yeah.

Fritzy: And I put some money in an envelope and sent it.

Frank: Oh, you did?

Fritzy: Yeah. In other words, I do one better.

Frank: That was nice of you.

Courtroom Banter

"Rico? I don't even know any fucking Rico!"

> —Colombo soldier Frank "The Beast" Falanga's courtroom outburst when informed that he had been indicted on RICO charges.

"It's a bullshit case."

> —Bonanno capo Vincent Asaro before a jury convicted him of perjury and fraud for lying on a driver's license application.

"I don't know how I wound up with that transactional immunity, but I did. That's the best kind of immunity you can get. In other words, when you've got transactional immunity, you can't be tried for anything you talk about. No matter what it is. But the Chicago judge gave me that kind of immunity. I walk out of court and the FBI guy says, 'I think the judge made a mistake.'"

> —Frank Cullotta.

"... Gene Gotti, John's slow-witted brother, who asked, when informed he was under arrest for violating the RICO statute, 'Say, who is this Mr. Rico, anyway?'"

—Eddie Maloney.

"They [Gotti's flunkies] continued expressing shock as Cutler, waving my rap sheet flamboyantly, informed the jury of my none-too-wholesome past. I had to force myself not to chuckle. Some of these guys had records that made me look like a boy scout in comparison."

—Eddie Maloney on testifying at the 1986/1987 Gotti trial.

"I feel like invoking Sister Marion's rule. Do you know what that is? I can clear half the courtroom if I invoke Sister Marion's rule. No chewing gum in class."

—Judge Raymond Dearie during the murder and racketeering trial of Luchese gangsters Michael and Robert Spinelli.

"No gum chewing, no candy eating, no face making of any sort will I tolerate once again."

—Dearie pressing his words a few minutes later when he saw a nephew of a witness glaring at the jury and making faces at them.

"You may have your authority, Mr. Krieger, and I have mine."

> —Judge I. Leo Glasser with the
> perfect retort to defense lawyer
> Albert Krieger during the racketeering
> and murder trial of John Gotti.

"Your Honor, that does it. I move to withdraw as counsel because after that ruling my client no longer needs the services of a lawyer; he needs the services of a pallbearer."

> —Jacques Schiffer, defense
> lawyer, after Judge Wilson
> refused to allow questions
> about a witness's character.

"What the hell are you talking about? He [the judge] didn't recess for our benefit. That son-of-a-bitch is going home to change his pants. That's the only reason he recessed."

> —Jimmy Hoffa after a gunman
> entered the courtroom and fired shots.

"… Carl DeLuna made the case for us in the end. He was an inverted, compulsive note taker. He kept notes on everything. Every twenty-dollar roll of quarters. Every trip. Every gas tank filled. He did it so that he could never be questioned about his expenses, because he would be able to show where the money went."

—Michael "Iron Mike" DeFeo, deputy director of the Justice Department's Organized Crime Strike Force, in 1978 on confirming the link between the mob, the Teamsters' Central States pension fund, and Las Vegas.

"Your Honor, you're getting to the core of the matter. There's no doubt about that. You're right there. If you go a little further, you could get the whole complete story."

—Steve "The Rifleman" Flemmi complimenting Judge Mark Wolf about his inquiry into corruption by FBI agents in Boston.

"Senior year, Your Honor."

—Gaetano "Tommy Horsehead" Scafidi when a judge asked him what year he graduated high school.

Sammy Bull Talks Nicknames at the John Gotti Trial

Federal Prosecutor John Gleeson: … you mention a term, you say "Nasabeak." What were you referring to?

Salvatore "Sammy Bull" Gravano: Paul.

Gleeson: Why Nasabeak? Why did you use that term?

Gravano: He's got a big nose.

***

Gleeson: Who did you understand [Gotti] to be referring to when he said "Jelly Belly"?

Gravano: At that point of the conversation, he's talking about Louie DiBono.

Gleeson: Is that a name that was used more than once for Louie DiBono?

Gravano: Yes.

Gleeson: Is that his nickname?

Gravano: No. Once we talk about killing him, we gave him a nickname of "Jelly Belly."

***

Gotti Lawyer Albert Krieger: Number four?

Gravano: Fat Sallie.

Krieger: By the way, Fat Sallie was fat, wasn't he?

Gravano: At one time in his life. Not at this particular point he wasn't too fat.

Krieger: Pardon?

Gravano: At one point in his life he was heavy, not at this point.

Krieger: He wasn't skinny then, was he?

Gravano: He wasn't really fat. The name stuck with him.

The Daily Grind

"Don't bring me no more fucking headaches, you hear. I don't want to hear about who robs who, who did this. Don't bring me no more headaches."

—Genovese capo Salvatore "Sammy Meatballs" Aparo to his crew.

"We got to resort to selling jewelry, imagine this fucking shit."

—Genovese soldier Vincent Aparo complaining about the depths to which the crew had sunk.

"I don't like the [prostitution] racket. What the hell. There's not enough dough in it for the risk we take."

—Lucky Luciano to associates James Frederico and Davie Betillo while they were partying in Chinatown with a Madam named Corky Flo.

"I'm sick of being shot at, sick of being trained around by a bunch of hyenas watching for a chance to kill me. If I go to a race track or drop out to see the greyhounds run, I don't know whether I'll get back alive. If I step into a joint to buy a pack of cigarettes it's even money I get a load of buckshot instead. Do you think I'd be fool enough to read a paper by a window in my own home? If I did, the chances are I'd be dead before I had time to glance over the headlines."

—Al Capone on the difficulty
of being Al Capone.

"You don't understand *Cosa Nostra. Cosa Nostra* means the boss is your boss. Boss is the boss is the boss. What I'm trying to say is a boss is a boss is a boss. What does a boss mean in this fuckin' thing. You might as well make anybody off the street."

—Gambino family underboss Neil
Dellacroce explaining a most important Mafia rule to soldiers John Gotti
and Angelo Ruggiero a few months
before he would die of natural
causes and they would team up to
kill their boss, Paul Castellano.

"Some days we hung around and did some gambling. There were other days we conspired to commit crimes."

—Gambino family associate Salvatore Polisi discussing time he spent with John Gotti at the Bergin Hunt and Fish Club during the late 1970s and early 1980s.

Money Ain't Everything

Legendary Mafia boss Simone "Sam the Plumber" DeCavalcante talking shop with soldier Bayonne Joe Zicarelli at DeCavalcante's base of operations, the Kenilworth Heating and Plumbing Company in Newark, New Jersey.

Bayonne Joe: Let me ask you a question—you're no dummy and neither am I. I've been around a long time. I've been stealing and knocking around since I was 12. Twelve years old! And I know one thing. I never brought my troubles to anybody! … I know what's going on with me. I'm on the razor's edge and I'm just lucky enough that I stay clean enough and I'm getting by. Most of the time I'm doing nothing. I take a ride, where do you think I go? I see my old man, I go see my wife, I go see my kids—I don't go no place. I stay away from people! I see you more than I see anybody in this whole thing. And when I go any place, I'm so careful! If anything turns up I wouldn't come. But these guys! Two agents were parked around the corner with New York plates one day. [I said]

'Hey do you know you brought the agents here?' [They said] 'So what? We ain't doing nothing.' [I said] 'Are you out of your mind? How do you know what I'm doing?

Sam the Plumber: That's right. How *do* they know what you're doing?

Bayonne Joe: They don't think the way we think. You ought to make a request to have me with you … under no captain. Just with you. What the hell, I'm from Jersey …. I guarantee I'd share everything with you.

Sam the Plumber: Listen, to hell with the money. I'd want you with me if we were the brokest guys in the world.

Death

"He's gone."

—Salvatore "Sammy Bull" Gravano
looking down at the body of Tommy
Bilotti in front of Sparks Steak House.

"Now they had $10,800 coming. So Nick died and that
little runt—that Italian guy—he said, 'Well, Nick
died—I guess we have to forget some money.' I said,
'Listen, you jerk. Nick didn't die—only his body is
dead! You guys are gonna get paid.' And by Christmas,
I brought them $10,800 to take care of everything."

—Simone "Sam the Plumber"
DeCavalcante on the
subject of one death.

"I'm only going out for a few minutes. Besides, I'm
wearing thermal underwear."

—Anthony "Tony Bender" Strollo,
rejecting his wife's suggestion to
put on an overcoat before going
out into the night forever.

Death

"If there's a life after death, I don't want to come back."

—Buddy Lansky,
son of Meyer Lansky.

"There is enough business for all of us without killing each other like animals in the streets. I don't want to die in the street punctured by machine-gun fire."

—Al Capone.

Once a Cocksucker, Always a Cocksucker

DeCavalcante crime family soldier Gaetano "Corky" Vastola and a partner in crime, Roulette Records President Morris Levy, got together to discuss the expected passing of acting boss Sonny Brocco, who was Vastola's cousin and their business associate.

Vastola: Sonny Brocco's dying.

Levy: Fuck him.

Vastola: He's dying. I went to see him at the hospital in isolation. He's in isolation.

Levy: When's he done nice things for people, Sonny Brocco? A lot of people are dying. Let me tell you something about me. If a guy's a cocksucker in his life, when he dies he don't become a saint.

Vastola: Yeah.

Levy: The only difference is, he was a live cocksucker Monday and he's a dead cocksucker Tuesday ....

Vastola: You're right. You're absolutely, 100 percent right.

"They just shoot themselves. The thing is, you mind your own business. You don't hear nothing. You don't see nothing."

—Bensonhurst, Brooklyn, resident,
after two corpses were found in a car.

"Growing up, all I ever wanted was to be like [Gambino mobster] Frank Scalise and die on the street with a gun in my hand."

—Anthony "Nino" Gaggi on
how he wanted to die.

"Everybody's gotta die sometime."

—John Gotti after his neighbor John
Favara, who had killed Gotti's son
Frank in a tragic car accident, had
disappeared and was believed dead.

"You heard of the double cross? In this business you gotta watch for the triple cross. You gotta always be alert. There's so much jealousy. Guys always trying to set you up, put you in traps. Trying to get ya killed."

—Nicholas "The Crow" Caramandi.

Death

"I will take it tomorrow, and I will be satisfied."

> —Bugsy Siegel after being
> sentenced to death.

"Just tell that rat [Abe] Reles I'll be waiting for him. Maybe it'll be in hell; I don't know. But I'll be waiting. And I bet I got a pitchfork."

> —Bugsy Siegel, to newspaper reporters
> after being sentenced to death.

"I don't want to go in there. I never killed nobody."

> —Bugsy, before getting
> into the electric chair.

"If a guy like that go to heaven there won't be anybody in hell."

> —Jesuit priest John A. Toomey, after
> Dutch Schultz was laid to rest with
> the rites of the Catholic Church.

"And whether we meet 'Schultz' in Heaven or not, there is one individual we are certain to encounter there; a gentleman who was in more or less the same line as 'Schultz'—the Thief who, as he was dying on Calvary asked the Man on the next Cross for forgiveness …"

> —John A. Toomey, S.J.

Frank & Fritzy: Only the Good Die Young

Fritzy, Frank, and his girlfriend Helen chat about their age and their appearance as time marches on.

Helen: Oh, it's hot, put some air conditioning on.

Frank: Get out, I'm freezing in here. Get out. I'll air conditioner you.

Fritzy: I could hear her.

Frank: She wants to put the air conditioner on, it's hot.

Fritzy: Yeah? You say you need a blanket.

Frank: [UI] I'm old! Whattya think? My bones are [UI]. She thinks I'm young.

Fritzy: You're old?

Frank: Yeah, I'm old. The bones, you know. You gotta watch it.

Helen: You're not old. Shut up.

Frank: She gets mad when I say that.

Helen: You're not old.

Frank: I'm gonna die soon. You won't have nobody.

Helen: Don't say that.

Fritzy: Marone, you hear. Don't say that.

Helen: Only the good die young. You ain't dying for a long time.

Fritzy: Ya hear?

Frank: Only the good die young.

Drugs

"I didn't know what I'm talking about, he didn't know what he was talking about. So he won't know that I don't know what I'm talking about."

>—John Gotti recounting how he and Joe Armone used to discuss Mafia business that they were not supposed to talk about—drugs.

"The most important thing in life is moderation. If cocaine becomes big in America it will be the downfall of this country, because the American people don't do things in moderation. Wait till the American people get hooked on cocaine—it will bring the country down to its knees."

>—Santo Trafficante explaining how cocaine brought down the Batista government.

"If I got pinched for junk, I would want to stay in jail ...."

>—Vincent "Fish" Cafaro on the serious consequences for Genovese family members who got caught violating the anti-drug dealing rule.

"In my FBI file, it says 'This man hates junk.' Right next to my picture."

—Benjamin "Lefty Guns" Ruggiero
about his feelings about heroin.

"I may do a lot of lousy things, but I'll never make a living off women or narcotics."

—Dutch Schultz.

"I robbed to support a drug habit. I murdered for money. It's two different things."

—Mob hitman John Veasey.

"Listen to me. In 45 hours they made 90 pinches. In 45 hours they made 90 pinches! You cannot beat them. They know the planes are going low. You cannot beat them. I'm telling you now, if you're putting up any money ..."

—Gambino soldier Angelo
Ruggiero telling drug partner
Edward Lino how sophisticated the
Drug Enforcement Administration
was in intercepting drug
smuggling planes.

"The most important part. Him and Chin made a pact, any friend of ours that gets pinched for junk, or that they even hear of anything about junk, they kill him. No administration meetings, no nothing, just go kill him. They're not warning nobody; not telling nobody because they feel the guy's gonna rat."

—Angelo Ruggiero telling Gene Gotti why they would be in big trouble if they were nailed for heroin dealing— their boss Paul Castellano and Genovese boss Vincent "Chin" Gigante had decreed capital punish- ment for family members who violated their no-drug-dealing rule.

Ego

"Here's what I'm saying now ... If you are to indict me, indict me in June so I can be tried over the August recess, [because] I don't want to miss any votes."

—Ohio Congressman James Traficant on timing his racketeering indictment.

"Nobody fucks with me."

—Vincent "Chin" Gigante to Correction Officer Christopher Sexton when the guard asked if any other inmates were bothering him.

"Listen carefully to me. You'll never see another guy like me if you live to be 5,000."

—John Gotti.

"Why do you think that this group of people fell apart without me? Everyone became their own boss, set their own moral codes, set their own reasons, their own rhymes, and that's the end of it ... that's the end of the ballgame."

—John Gotti.

Ego

"Who's gonna challenge me? Who's gonna defy me? What are they gonna do? Take a shot? Like I did to the other guy? I'd welcome that. I'll kill their fuckin' mothers, their fathers."

—John Gotti.

"There's only one boss. And that's me."

—Nicodemo "Little Nicky" Scarfo, Philadelphia mob boss, to his associates.

"For Christ's sake. I'm national now. Maybe not a hero, but they know Capone everywhere."

—Al Capone, when it was suggested that he could become a national hero if he went on tour as a reformed evangelist.

"Even as a little boy, I remember swearing to myself that when I grew up I'd be very rich, and I'd make sure that for the rest of her days my mother had only the best."

—Meyer Lansky.

"Ego, ego is a dangerous thing ... if you put power in the wrong hands."

—Joe Sodano.

"Let them come. I'm not afraid of anybody."

—Dutch Schultz.

"There is no sitting Commission right now. The biggest family in New York is the Chin's family … they can go fuck themselves … There's only one boss in Philadelphia … and that's Ralph Natale and that's where the fuck it's at."

—Philadelphia boss Ralph Natale
before he became the first Mafia
boss to cooperate with the feds.

"I wouldn't stay in that jail another night if they gave me the place. Who do they think I am? Some poor punk? Well, I'm not. I'm a big shot. I've got some mighty important business that needs attention."

—Dutch Schultz.

"Any guy who can lick the government can lick anybody."

—Dutch Schultz.

"This tough world ain't no place for dunces. And you can tell those smart guys in New York that the Dutchman is no dunce and as far as he is concerned Alcatraz doesn't exist. I'll never see Alcatraz. Al Capone was a dunce for going to Alcatraz."

—Dutch Schultz.

"Well, he finds little things. He snips the hair in my nose and ears, he snips this and that."

—John Gotti, telling Salvatore "Sammy Bull" Gravano why he got his hair washed, cut, and blown dry every day.

 Frank & Fritzy: It's Good for Ya

Fritzy: Did you eat?

Frank: Had some chicken soup.

Fritzy: Again?

Frank: Yup.

Fritzy: Why don't ya have a piece of fish?

Frank: I like the soup.

Fritzy: I know you like that, but that's no good for ya …

Frank: Vegetables and everything.

Fritzy: Makes you fart a lot.

Family

"Boss? No boss. He's boss of the toilet. My son is sick. Boss of shit. Six years he lives here with me. Every day I care for him. I feed him, I wash him, I cry over him."

> —Vincent "Chin" Gigante's mom before he threw in the towel and admitted fooling doctors into thinking he was crazy.

"I know my brother very well. My brother was a street kid but to label him as a boss of a conglomerate that extorts is ridiculous. He didn't run anything because he couldn't run anything."

> —Rev. Louis Gigante, before brother Chin Gigante admitted running things for the Genovese crime family.

"What do you need a list for? I don't understand that. For posterity? To show that [he] went shopping one time?"

> —John Gotti voicing disbelief that his son Junior kept lists of crime family members that were seized by authorities in a raid.

Family

"My father is the last of the Mohicans."

> —Victoria Gotti describing her dad
> after he was found guilty of all counts.

"Go against your cousin. Go against your own uncles. Fuck you think you're kidding? Love nobody. Who do you think you're fuckin' kidding?"

> —John Gotti.

"I got to get one [hearts] for my sister, one for my father, I mean one for my mother ... my sister and my mother. And then I get one for my father to my sister and my mother. And then I got to get one for my wife ... I got to buy my father's Valentine's Day hearts, too. You imagine that? He lost his job now."

> —Genovese soldier
> Vincent "Vinny" Aparo.

"I don't know why anyone would want to bring his son into the life."

> —Chin Gigante's response
> when John Gotti said his son
> Junior had just been "made."

"Fear? Is that what this is about? Showing fear? You're going to walk in there and let them stick a gun to the back of your head and blow your brains out so you won't be accused by some punk of showing fear? You're going to let them kill me, your son, just because you don't want to show fear?"

—Michael "The Yuppie Don" Franzese to his father Sonny.

"I was sick! We didn't even get a reward. I think the bank guy said something about my father being rewarded in life."

—Salvatore "Sammy Bull" Gravano's reaction when his father insisted they return $500 to a local bank that they had received due to a bank error.

"So in the meantime, my daughter she working with me, too ... Sal, I wish she was a boy. Because she's intelligent, smart, and she no take no baloney from nobody. And special, see ... how they acted and she hated their guts, you know. The other day, you know what she told me, she said, 'Daddy ... I gonna spit in their faces'."

—Philadelphia mob boss John Stanfa.

Family

"It's my whining brother-in-law Eddie, a whining
motherfucker all my life, who puts the idea in my head.
He's caused me nothing but trouble with his devious
ways, always looking for the angle. A couple of guys in
my crew wanted to whack him. You can't trust him,
they said. But he's got a big edge with me. His wife is
my sister and I ain't ever going to hurt her, even
though he's treating her like shit. He double crosses
me. You know, it's like when you're kids standing by the
edge of the pool, and it's one, two, three, jump!
Schmucko jumped, and he didn't."

> —Sammy Bull Gravano describing
> the circumstances of how he came
> to cooperate with the feds.

"What business have you got going around telling my
relatives I killed thirteen people?"

> —Sam "Momo" Giancana after
> discovering that FBI agent
> Ralph Hill informed his aunt,
> Rose Flood, about the murders.

"I want you to understand that La Cosa Nostra comes
before anything. You are now on call twenty-four hours
a day. There are no excuses. If your mother is sick on
her deathbed, and the family calls, you leave your
mother and come."

> —Thomas DiBella, acting boss
> of the Colombo family, to The
> Yuppie Don Franzese after his
> induction into the crime family.

"I let my kids down and feel bad about it. I'm unhappy with myself. I wanted to stay close. I wanted them to live comfortable, but between prison and the thieving attorneys, it didn't work out."

—Turncoat Colombo capo
The Yuppie Don Franzese.

"I never touch drugs. I don't believe in that. I no gamble. My favorite sport is hunting … my family come first before any sports or anything, because I want to make sure my family got food on the table."

—John Stanfa.

"Boss of this, boss of that … the 'family.' What family? I was Sonny's family. My children were his family. Sometimes when I read the papers, I thought he had another wife and kids somewhere, because they were always talking about his family, and it wasn't us."

—Tina, John "Sonny" Franzese's wife.

"You are no better or worse than anyone else in La Cosa Nostra. You are your own man. You and your father are now equals. Your father, sons, and brothers have no priority. We are all as one, united in blood. Once you become part of this, there is no greater bond."

—Colombo family acting boss
Thomas DiBella on the Mafia way.

Family

"In a family, it's like a chain. You keep breaking the beads, forget about it."

—Anthony Piccolo, Stanfa's
crime family consigliere.

"If I do something, then I deserve to pay the penalty. But the FBI shouldn't harass my children and relatives because of what I do."

—Joe Colombo on why he
was picketing the FBI.

"You can't be more disappointed than I am in my family, utterly impossible. If I could go home, I say it right out, I wouldn't go near them with a ten-foot long fucking pole."

—John Gotti complaining to
brother Peter about his son
Junior's failings as acting boss.

"My fuckin' brother has nine lives."

—John Gotti, after hearing that his
brother Gene was free on bail
after a drug conviction.

"Normal. Normal in this family is terrifying, that's for sure. Normal in this family is terrifying."

—John Gotti discussing his
relatives with brother Peter.

"So, what's the story with Carmine? Is he feeling good? Is he not feeling good? Is his medication increased? Decreased? Is it up? Down? Does he get in the back seat of the car and think someone has stolen the steering wheel?"

> —John Gotti asking his daughter
> Victoria about her husband
> Carmine, a Gambino soldier
> with emotional problems.

"He watches television and he drives."

> —Tore Bonanno, Salvatore "Bill"
> Bonanno's young son, answering a
> friend of the family's questions
> about his father's occupation.

"OK, you play the mommy ... you play the daddy ... and I'll play Carl."

> —Tore Bonanno, Bill Bonanno's
> young son, quickly adjusting to having
> bodyguard Carl Simari hanging
> around the house for protection.

"I ate from the same table as Albert and came from the same womb but I know he killed many men and he deserved to die."

> —Anthony "Tough Tony" Anastasio
> to detectives after his brother Albert
> was killed in a midtown-Manhattan
> hotel barbershop.

My Wife Would Make More Money If She Didn't Work

Fritzy: So, meantime, meantime, it costs me, my wife goes to work, makes a hundred. It costs me three hundred to send her.

Frank: Three hundred to send her? Why?

Fritzy: It costs, if I tell ya what it costs me to get her off goin', back and forth, forget it, it's a joke. Ya know?

Frank: She goes with a private car?

Fritzy: She goes with her own car. She parks in the parking lot.

Frank: She made a hundred dollars, so she …

Fritzy: She made a hundred dollars.

Frank: She parks in a parking lot, there's money there. And then, the …

Fritzy: The lunch. What about the lunches every day?

Frank: And lunches every day.

Fritzy: And the train, back and forth from, uh, from the parking lot she takes the train for three min, five minutes.

Frank: And then she takes the train from …

Fritzy: That's two dollars.

Frank: Uh-huh.

Fritzy: Uh, $15 a week, that's 17. The lunch is five dollars a day, another 30.

Frank: Uh-huh.

Fritzy: She made a hundred dollars last week.

Frank: That's all?

Fritzy: That's all.

Frank: I thought she'd a make big money.

Fritzy: Later on.

Frank: Yeah.

Fritzy: Later on. Not now. They're training her now, ya know?

Frank: Yeah, you wanna get her back. [UI] think you want her in the field, huh.

Fritzy: In the field? Where? What field?

Frank: Oh, where she's workin'. In the field, she'll be then. Then you don't want her there, huh?

Fritzy: Ah. I don't, I just, I just want her, she's gotta …

Frank: [UI] there. She'll start to look beautiful and then, then, gleamin' again.

Fritzy: Lemme …

Frank: Then you get the guys go, "Hello, how are you …"

Fritzy: She's got a glow already. She's already glow, she looks good already glowin'.

Frank: They got the big eyes over there, ya know?

Fritzy: What big eyes? Big eyes.

Frank: You better watch.

Fritzy: She's a grandmother. What is she gonna?

Frank: I know the grandmother. You never know.

Fritzy: Yeah.

Frank: A little drinkin', a little, a little, uh …

Fritzy: Yeah, well, if they wanna rob her, they could have her. You ever hear that guy, "Take my, take my wife, please," he goes. What's his name, the comedian?

Gambling

"All I'm interested in is the gambling. It would be different if I sold broads."

> —Joseph "Joey Doves" Aiuppa drawing the line at being labeled a pimp.

"Nice carpet ya got here kid. Be good for a crap game."

> —Crazy Joe Gallo on walking into the office of chief counsel Robert Kennedy in the late 1950s.

"That's all. I ain't going crazy no more."

> —John Gotti to his bookie after placing a hunch-bet of only $500 on a horse whose name he liked, John Q. Arab.

"A big game that everybody was playing was trying to figure out who the different characters were supposed to be. There was one character I had no problem recognizing: the horse who had his head cut off. I think I bet on him out at Aqueduct the day before I saw the movie."

> —Joey the Hitman.

"The camper stopped because there was a sign outside that said LUNCH, 49¢—24 HOURS A DAY. The guy came in for a cheap lunch and started playing blackjack. He left behind twenty-four hundred dollars while I was sitting there. He never even got to Vegas. He just put his family back in the camper and went home."

—Frank "Lefty" Rosenthal.

"I grew up reading the racing form. I used to tear it apart. I knew everything there was to know about the form. I used to read it in class. I was a tall, skinny, shy kid. I was six foot one when I was a teenager and I was kind of withdrawn. I was sort of a loner, and horse racing was my challenge."

—Lefty Rosenthal.

The Incredible Shrinking Head

John Gotti interrupts a telephone conversation about gambling with his buddy Angelo Ruggiero to rave about a television program he's watching.

John: I just watched them shrink a head!

Angelo: Shrink whose head?

John: The Amazons, creatures of the Amazons.

Angelo: Yeah?

John: They didn't show you capturing the guy, they just show you his head. Forget about it.

Angelo: Yeah? I got to go watch it.

Gambling

"But I really learned gambling in the bleachers of Wrigley Field and Comiskey Park. There were about two hundred guys up there every game and they bet on everything. Every pitch. Every swing. Everything had a price. There were guys shouting numbers at you. It was great. It was an open-air casino. Constant action."

—Lefty Rosenthal.

"George and Sam were independent operators, but they still had to pay protection. All the card rooms and bookie rooms paid off in those days. Bookmakers took care of the cops and they took care of the Outfit. And sometimes the Outfit took care of the cops. In the end, everybody could wind up taking care of everybody, just as long as everybody made money."

—Lefty Rosenthal.

"But in the end, the odds are built against you. When I was a kid in Chicago I always heard them say, 'In the winter, the bookies go to Florida and the players eat snowballs.'"

—Lefty Rosenthal.

"Benny made millions and millions as a bookmaker and Benny couldn't tell you who Joe DiMaggio played for. I'm serious."

—Lefty Rosenthal.

"The bank wrote them a letter and told them that they would close out his account unless they had a truck to handle the money. So he bought a truck."

—Warren Olney III, California attorney general, explaining how bringing in the money from gaming ships became a problem.

"Bartenders don't drink because they see the consequences. I know how the odds are stacked against the players. You can't beat the casinos."

—Santo Trafficante explaining why he does not gamble.

"Gambling pulls at the core of a man."

—Meyer Lansky.

"If you say that I'm a gambler, you will be right. But I am an uncommon gambler. An uncommon gambler is a man who accommodates common gamblers."

—Frank Costello to New York newspaperman Bob Considine.

"There's no such thing as a lucky gambler. There are just the winners and the losers. The winners are those who control the game."

—Meyer Lansky.

Gambling

"Baseball's all fuckin' streaks man … That's all baseball is, it's fuckin' streaks.

> —Tommy Marrone berating a gambler for betting on baseball.

"It's a sucker's game. You can't win out there, you understand. We got the percentages rigged all in our favor. The longer you stay, the more you play, the more chance you got of losing. I don't let nobody around me who gambles. A couple thousand, okay, but no gambling!"

> —Outfit associate Gus Alex when he learned that the owner of a tailor shop had gone out to Las Vegas and lost $20,000 gambling.

 Frank & Fritzy: Ante Up

A pal of Fritzy's gets roped into a rigged card game at the Triangle Social Club (where boss Vincent "Chin" Gigante always seemed to hold the winning hand and is never in danger of some Wild West–style justice).

Fritzy: Marone, I hear they, they, they initiated my friend there, they sat him down over there. They made him play cards. The other guy got him.

Frank: I saw him yesterday.

Fritzy: Yeah, they got him playing cards …

Frank: Didn't you wise that guy up not to [UI] play cards.

Fritzy: What?

Frank: Didn't you tell him?

Fritzy: Hey, he's the one. Joe Bozo got it. Joey says, "Alright, sit down." He says, "Uh, you wanna play, you wanna try?" "Yeah, okay."

Frank: That's the end.

Fritzy: I says, "Wait ..."

Frank: But it cost him 120, 200, 300 ...

Fritzy: Yeah, not too bad, he went for $60 yesterday.

Frank: That's the beginning.

Fritzy: He [Chin] gave 'em the sympathy act. He patted 'em on the back, the other guy. "Geez, ya really had bad hands, huh?" He patted 'em, you know, "Yeah, boy you really did wind up ..."

Frank: Does he know he ain't got a chance there with the thief?

Fritzy: That's the, that's the No Chance Saloon.

Frank: If that was the days of the West, he [Chin] woulda been dead. They woulda shot him under the table.

Fritzy: Forget about it. They'da taken pictures of him shot up in the coffin outside, and everybody would take, uh, for a quarter, a nickel apiece they take pictures of the guy.

Frank: Yeah.

Health

"The doctor started giving her some mumbo-jumbo medical doubletalk that I had a rare disease. He told her that if I had intercourse, I could drop dead at any moment."

—Santo Trafficante, who was having an affair, describing how his doctor deceived his wife Josie.

"Every once in a while I would pretend I wanted to have intercourse with Josie. I would beg her, but she would get all upset and talk me out of it—that it was too dangerous."

—Santo Trafficante.

"All he doing is examine my eye, take pictures and I keep getting billed. I don't care about the bill because I ain't paying them. But if you are doing it for that don't make me come, just put it in."

—Genovese capo Salvatore "Sammy Meatballs" Aparo on going to the eye doctor.

"Sure, if I was out on the street, they'd tell me I got two weeks to live. I'm doing life, so it's benign."

> —Gambino capo Robert "Bobby Cabert" Bisaccia about the good news he received after a biopsy.

"He coined his own name for the morphine and whenever he wanted another shot he would manage a smile, somehow, and say, 'How about another bon bon, Doc?'"

> —Dr. Charles Calasibetta on caring for Dutch Schultz after he was shot.

"Alright. I felt worse and I felt better."

> —John Gotti describing to lawyer Mike Coiro how he felt.

"What did I tell you the other day? I'm tired, I'm tired. But I'll always be me. I'll always be me until the day I die."

> —John Gotti to daughter Victoria, as they discussed how his son and her husband were following him into prison.

"I'm sick, Frankie, and I ain't got no right to be sick. I'm not goin' partying. I'm not going to [race]tracks, [or] popping girls. I'm not doing nothin' selfish here."

> —John Gotti to Frank Locascio.

"You know what I want you to do, Frank? We gotta both buy chemotherapy with the money I got."

—John Gotti telling Frank Locascio how they should spend all his money.

 Frank & Fritzy Crack a Back

Frank: Yeah.

Fritzy: Okay, now I got that whole, my son has got that whole plank where ya, where ya hang on top and then you dangle, ya know?

Frank: That's good for ya ….

Fritzy: Okay, but let me tell ya what I done. I tried it about four, five times. Nothin' worked, ya know, I hung [UI]. I hurt, I laid down. Nothin' really fuckin' worked. So what I did, then I had gotten sick, ya know my fuckin' [UI], I don't know, one thing on top of the other was goin'. Now, I told my wife, "Look," 'cause after Jerry the Rubber was tellin' me about they got a new thing, a harness, like they put instead of you turnin' upside down they put your body in a harness and you hang, like, uh, just in midair.

Frank: Hmm.

Fritzy: I says, "But that don't sound right." I says, "What's gonna pull the fuckin' weight?" [UI] when you put weight legs. Ya know, legs on your weight. I mean, uh, weights on your legs. I, I, says ya know what? I got the treadmill downstairs, ya know, and the big, big bar comes on top where you hang on, where you put your hands in front of you when you're walkin', ya know? I said I'm gonna get the gravity shoes, and I'm gonna, like, put it on that bar and then sit on the floor instead of hangin' all the way down. Least my head is level and my feet like I'm in, I'm in traction. So now I put the, my two feet up, I got two of the bars that I, I could pull on. I put, like I really, like I'm puttin' force to stretch my legs. The way you would crack your fingers in a knuckle, ya know?

Frank: Yeah.

Fritzy: And I'm pushin', all of a sudden I hear "bump-a-crack." … And I, so I kept, ya know, the pressure on for about 10 minutes, 15 minutes. I told my wife 'cause she was there when she heard the crack 'cause she, she hooked me up. I got off. Not a fuckin' pain, Frank.

Frank: Uh-huh.

Honesty

"Honest people don't have no ethics."

> —Simone "Sam the
> Plumber" DeCavalcante.

"You can't cheat an honest man."

> —Nicholas "The Crow" Caramandi.

"Sometimes people give you more information by lying to you than by telling you the truth."

> —Organized Crime Strike Force
> Prosecutor Marvin Rudnick.

"But one thing I ain't gonna be is two-faced. I'm gonna call 'em like I see 'em. That I gotta do 'til the day I die."

> —John Gotti.

"You show me a fucking guy that's greedy, and I'll rob him. No matter how, I'll find a way to rob him. Because if he's got greed in him, there's always a way."

> —The Crow Caramandi.

"Tell Jimmy that there is no reason for us to meet so long as we have you [he emphasized 'you']. Because if I ever get called before a grand jury or an investigating committee, I want to be able to raise my hand and swear under oath that I never met Jimmy Hoffa, without committing perjury."

—Santo Trafficante telling lawyer
Frank Ragano why he didn't want
to meet Jimmy Hoffa.

"I wouldn't take it [the money], Frankie. I'm not a goon. I'm not a grease ..."

—John Gotti.

"Toddo was an honest man within the life. It may be hard to understand that. He was a gangster and a crook, but to us he had honor. You hear the expression about honor among thieves. Well, some thieves do have honor among thieves."

—Salvatore "Sammy Bull" Gravano
about the honesty of his mentor,
Toddo Marino.

"The man did what he had to do and he knew how to do it. He did it the right way. If there was a dollar to cut up, he cut it up fifty-fifty, not sixty-forty."

—Sam Pontarelli on Al Capone.

"If there is one thing that we who are from Naples must always remember, it is that if you hang out with a Sicilian for twenty years and you have trouble with another Sicilian, the Sicilian that you hung out with all that time will turn on you. In other words, you can never trust them."

—Wiseguy Alessandro Vollero
telling fellow Neapolitan Joe
Valachi about Sicilians.

"The game is so unpredictable, you never know what's gonna happen. Today he's your friend, tomorrow he wants to kill ya. You can't trust nobody."

—The Crow Caramandi.

"You're called to the grand jury. You gotta take the Fifth. All right so far? Now they give you immunity. What do you do? There is three things: common sense is one part, 75% of the answers. Another 10% or 15%, you gotta dance and bob and weave—one, I didn't remember, I don't think so, or to the best of my knowledge. Okay? Let's say 15%, so we're up to 90%. Ten percent, you out and out lie."

—Sammy Bull Gravano on how to
testify before a grand jury.

Incredible
Explanations

"The way of life I and my friends had chosen was but a means to attain social advancement and respectability. We didn't consider ourselves criminals."

—Joe Bonanno justifying his way of life.

"At the time of my guilty plea in 1994, I was retired. I am still retired. I have no intentions of ever coming out of retirement."

—Luchese capo Salvatore Avellino
in a futile attempt to get some
time off his federal prison time.

"Because of the name he uses—Trafficante. One who traffics in illegal drugs—that's what the name means in Spanish."

—Cuban official citing evidence
that Trafficante is a drug trafficker.

"If you're going to judge him by his name, then he's a saint, since Santo, in Italian, means saint."

—Frank Ragano, defense lawyer,
responding to Cuban official.

"It was the monthly payment. We're getting too old to go down to the library every time we have an argument and need to find out the answer. So we got together to buy a set of *Encyclopedia Britannica.* The young man was the salesman."

> —Benny Sigelbaum, a cohort of
> Meyer Lansky, when asked about a
> check he gave a young businessman
> who had met with Lansky.

You're What?

Cammy Franzese: Mom, I think I'm pregnant again.

Mom: How can you be? You just had a baby. You're not supposed to have sex for six weeks.

Cammy: My husband was going to jail. I'm supposed to say no?

"I burned it on a piece of roast beef."

> —Al Capone's explanation for the
> bandage on his right hand, a result
> of drunken behavior at a party.

"Those other times, I was a witness at my own trials. I had to try and get away with it."

> —Abe Reles, testifying as a prosecution
> witness, explaining why he'd never
> before told the truth under oath.

"You got to remember I was just getting over that bullet in the head, and I wasn't thinking too good."

> —Joseph Valachi, on why he made
> a dumb move that led cops to his
> door after a robbery.

"Every time the cops started one of their supposed clean-ups and all, they'd send some cop over to wherever I was located and they'd charge me with anything. Then some A&P clerk would come and identify me for some stickup just to get their name in the papers, and next day I'd be turned out. That's how come I got a record."

> —Dutch Schultz explaining
> his arrest record.

"It's the Devil eating his body."

> —Mafia boss Frank Salemme describing facial tics and spasms that informant Steve "The Rifleman" Flemmi developed in prison.

"I'm no public enemy. I'm a public benefactor."

> —Dutch Schultz.

"He had no income."

> —J. Richard Davis, Dutch Schultz's lawyer on Schultz not filing tax returns for three years.

"I think they've picked me out—the government. I mean—because a certain group of individuals, some of them still in the government and some actually prosecuting this case, had a personal grudge against me. And they wanted the publicity out of it, too. That was mostly it."

—Dutch Schultz.

"I offered $100,000 when the government was broke and people were talking revolution and they turned me down cold. You can see how that at least I was willing to pay. Everybody knows I am being persecuted in this case. I wanted to pay. They were taking it from everybody else, but they wouldn't take it from me. I tried to do my duty as a citizen—maybe I'm not a citizen?"

—Dutch Schultz.

"If you lock up the jury, they're going to hold it against me, because if I wasn't charged they wouldn't be locked up."

—Jimmy Hoffa shouting after hearing at a strategy meeting a recommendation that his jury be sequestered.

Oops ...

Billy D'Elia: The answer was that when he [Carmine Franco] was standing by the [trash] trucks, somebody should have bumped him in and let them compact him.

Sal Profaci: Of course this might have caused some problems with the Genovese organization.

D'Elia: You know what they say in New York, don't you?

Profaci: Accidents happen.

D'Elia: Oops, we didn't know.

Profaci: Oops is right. Shame on us.

Labor Racketeering

"It's always a good popular play for the Government to go after racketeers. It keeps folks' minds off bank closings and widows and orphans being swindled."

—Dutch Schultz.

"All these bullshit critics keep saying we're connected to the mob. Let me tell you something, Frank. Without them the Teamsters wouldn't be where we are today. I couldn't have done it without them …. I decided to use the mob and they've used me. But I've used them for the benefit of the rank and file and I believe I've used them more than they've used me. Chrissakes, anybody thinks you can run a fucking union like the Teamsters without the help of the mob has got to be stupid."

—Jimmy Hoffa.

"If you already think you've got enough insurance fine. I hear you're having a labor problem? Bad one, huh? I'm sorry. Ask around, you might get some ideas about how to solve the problem."

—Precinct captain of the first ward
soliciting an owner to buy "insurance."

"When Courtney was state's attorney and all of us guys got indicted and Nitti was hollerin' like hell, we broke through and we got the assistant state's attorney and we got the witness and let me tell you I had the jury, too, just in case. That's the way we got to revert to these days."

—Murray "Hump" Humphrey
referring to 1940 when he was
indicted with Fred Evans and
Frank Nitti for extortion of the
Bartenders Union.

"Everything has to be inferior materials. When I need four wires, I put three. Twenty nails, I put 10 …. We're not building the pyramids. If it only lasts five years, that's not a problem …. Cosmetically, it'll look good."

—Philadelphia boss Ralph Natale
on how he intended to make
money on some government
building contracts.

"You gotta control the workers. Right now you control the employers. You got to control the men. That's the power."

> —Mob-connected private sanitation executive Emidio "Mimi" Fazzini discussing the economics of the Long Island garbage business with Luchese capo Salvatore Avellino.

"Right. Right now, we as the association, we control the bosses. Now when we control the men, we control the bosses even better, now because they're even more fuckin' afraid …. Now when you got a guy that steps out of line and this and that you got the whip. You got the fuckin' whip. This is what [Luchese boss Antonio "Tony Ducks" Corallo] tells me all the time: 'A strong union makes money for everybody, including the wiseguys.' The wiseguys make even more money with a strong union."

> —Salvatore Avellino expanding on Fazzini's assessment with some special insight from family boss Antonio "Tony Ducks" Corallo.

"Bust him up."

> —Gambino boss John Gotti ordering his crew to assault carpenters' union official John O'Connor after his workers trashed a family-owned restaurant in a labor dispute.

"We could cause you problems, number one. Number two, think of it like this. You gotta pay LILCO [Long Island Lighting Company]. You gotta pay your fuckin' electric bill, right? You gotta pay your phone bill. You gotta pay your fuckin' rent. And you gotta pay us."

—Gambino associate Carl Kline explaining the costs of doing business to the proprietor of an adult entertainment porn shop on Long Island.

Las Vegas Musings

"Jay would take four months off a year and just go up and down the state opening slots. All he had to do was look at a machine and it would give up the drop. He loved doing it. I've seen him open ice machines at gas stations just for the pleasure of seeing the quarters roll out."

> —Ted Lynch describing George Jay Vandermark as the greatest slots cheat who had ever lived.

"You dumb son of a bitch, you're gonna get us all in trouble. We can't steal that much."

> —George Jay Vandermark.

"I'm highly disciplined."

> —Casino operator Allen Glick about his uncanny ability to keep still and not move a muscle for extended periods.

"As he talked, Glick sat very still. Very controlled. You'd get a businessman's answer to everything you asked. He was like a zombie. A nonperson. And the mirrors all around the room were reflecting the same nonperson. After a while I began to wonder which of these guys was the real Glick."

—Homicide chief, Beecher Avants, after interviewing Allen Glick, a mob-connected Las Vegas entrepreneur.

"If you excluded everybody with something in their backgrounds from getting licensed, you'd probably have to terminate fifty percent of the people in this town."

—Allen Glick testifying before the Gambling Control Board, Las Vegas.

"There is no casino, in this country at least, that is capable of defending itself against a skim. There are no safeties. You can't prevent a skim if a guy knows what he's doing."

—Frank "Lefty" Rosenthal.

"An organized skim calls for at least no less than three people. At a high level. You cannot do it without. You just can't do it. If there's a way, I'd like someone to tell me how, because he would have an exclusive patent on it."

—Lefty Rosenthal.

"… everybody in Las Vegas who's got any brains is on the hustle. Nobody lives off their paycheck parking cars or dealing cards. That's the thing about Las Vegas. Everybody sharp who lives there is on the make. That's why they're there."

—Lefty Rosenthal.

"It should have been so sweet. Everything was in place. We were given paradise on earth, but we fucked it all up."

—Frank Cullotta on Las Vegas.

"I remembered the oft-told story of a guy arriving in a $30,000 Jaguar and departing in a $200,000 bus."

—Mob associate Eddie Maloney describing Las Vegas.

"This fuckin' joint robs you WITHOUT a gun."

—Maloney cohort Richard "Richie" Chaisson in a casino.

"Well, originally I spelled it the same way as the hotel in Miami Beach: Fontainebleau. But then I got a letter from them putting me on notice that they were going to sue me for using their name. So I dropped one *e* and spelled it 'Fontainbleau.'"

—Zachary "Red" Strate, developer, explaining how he got away with calling his hotel the Fontainbleau.

Law Enforcement

"They know everything under the sun. They know who's back of it, they know amici [made men], they know capodecina [family captains], they know there is a Commission [Mafia ruling body]. We got to watch right now, this thing, where it goes and stay as quiet as possible."

—Stefano Magaddino, Buffalo Mafia chief talking about the feds.

"I wish they were bringing him back in a box. That's what the bum was afraid of—that he'd be brought in dead. That's why he surrendered. The trail was getting too hot for him."

—United States commissioner Lester T. Hubbard on Dutch Schultz's surrender.

"It is a sad commentary on the police department of every city in which Schultz had been hiding."

—New York City Mayor Fiorello La Guardia after Dutch Schultz's surrender.

"They're overgrown bullies. They're too lazy to work—that's New York cops I'm talking about."

> —Dutch Schultz expressing
> his feelings about cops.

"This is like Nazi Germany and I'm the biggest Jew in the country."

> —Sam "Momo" Giancana referring
> to Bobby Kennedy's investigation
> of the Chicago family boss.

"All right deal me in. If they want to play checkers, we'll play chess. Fuck them."

> —James "Whitey" Bulger after
> accepting the FBI's offer
> to become an informant.

"His job was to protect us."

> —Steve Flemmi describing FBI
> agent John Connolly's role.

"These guys like you and will do anything for you. If there's anything you ever need, just ask, and they will do it."

> —FBI agent John Connolly to his
> boss John Morris referring to
> informants Whitey Bulger
> and Steve Flemmi.

Who Do You Trust?

Salvatore "Sammy Bull" Gravano, describing his removal from the Metropolitan Correctional Center in Manhattan after he made his deal to cooperate with the FBI:

They bring me out to where Bruce Mouw and the other FBI agents are waiting. Just then, this black woman comes by. She's a guard and she patrols the perimeter of the jail. As I'm coming out, she looks at all the agents, and she looks at me, and she says, "Oh no, Sammy. Not you."

I said, "Yeah, it's me." I was literally sick to my stomach. It killed me inside.

Mouw walks over and shakes my hand. He opened a car door, and I got in. I told him, "Are you Mouw?" He says, "Yes," and I said, "I heard you were from Iowa."

He said that was right and I said, "Well, if I got to trust somebody, it might as well be somebody from Iowa." And off we went.

"He became a fuckin' liability. You can never have the top guy as an informant. You have the top guy, he's making policy, and then he owns you. He owns you."

—Bob Fitzpatrick, former FBI
agent, talking about Whitey
Bulger and the FBI.

"I won't do that. The government is turning everyone into rats. It'll become Russia. Every other day they call me: 'You wanna go with Chico?'"

> —Boston money launderer Jimmy
> Katz refusing to follow the lead of
> turncoat Chico Krantz and cut a
> deal with the feds.

"Handling informants was kind of like a circus. If the circus is going to work you need to have a guy in there with the lions and tigers."

> —FBI agent John Connolly
> talking about the difficulty
> of the job he performed.

"The best definition of Christmas I ever heard came from out West, where some professionals were testing gangsters with the Binet test. One of the questions they asked was, 'What is Christmas?' and the answer was, 'Something a cop thinks about every day.'"

> —Dutch Schultz.

"It turns out one of the stakeout guys, the cop who shot Tony, had grown up in his neighborhood and knew Tony Esposito and his family. And it was just a fluke thing that he and his stakeout team were working there that day .... When the guy pulled Tony's mask off and seen Tony, he started to cry. It was something."

> —Nicholas "The Crow" Caramandi,
> describing a busted bank robbery.

"Yeah, but this time they got a real tough one. Put you to bed and take you out. They don't leave you go. Terrific drive they got on. They're on a lot of people that way. I'm telling you. I'm having my troubles."

—Murray "Hump" Humphrey
talking about problems the new
FBI's Top Hoodlum Program was
causing him and his associates.

"It was ironic that a man guilty of inciting hundreds of murders, in some of which he took a personal hand, had to be punished merely for failure to pay taxes on the money he had made by murder."

—FBI Director J. Edgar
Hoover on Al Capone.

"Maybe we should think FBI. Those bimbos try so hard to blend in though, they stick out like fucking sore thumbs."

—Richard Chaisson describing FBI
agents to Eddie Maloney.

Lawyers

"You guys go to dinner and get a few belts of idiot juice in you and at night you roar like lions. But the next morning when we get to court and the idiot juice has worn off, you're as meek as goddamn lambs."

—Jimmy Hoffa berating his lawyers
for not being aggressive.

"These are rats. They all want their money up front. And then, you get four guys that want 65, 75 thousand a piece, up front. You're talking about three hundred thousand in one month .... Where we going here?"

—John Gotti complaining about
his lawyers, who included Gerald
Shargel, Bruce Cutler, John
Pollok, and Edwin Schulman.

"This is what bothers me. I paid $135,000 for their appeal—for Joe Gallo and Joe Piney's appeal. I paid thousands of dollars to Pollok. That was not for me. I paid $17,500 for printing. I just got hit with another $12,800 for printing. That's $170,000 for printing these fucking minutes and [to] prepare briefs, whatever you fucking call 'em."

—John Gotti complaining about his lawyers.

"Then I gave 'em $25,000 for Carneg's [John Carneglia's] appeal. That's what I told him [Shargel] last night: 'I gave youse $300,000 in one year … Before youse made a court appearance, youse got $40,000, $35,000 and $25,000. That's without counting John Pollok. He's brand new on the scene.' They each need backup lawyers. He needs that Schulman, that little guy. He's gonna get $5,000 a week …."

—John Gotti complaining about his lawyers.

"I needed to pull heists to pay an attorney to defend me on a previous heist."

—Tough Guy Eddie Maloney.

"I retained Joseph Prado, a short, pot-bellied wiseguy attorney who seemed to represent everybody on Mulberry Street. Prado, an early day Bruce Cutler [Gotti's lawyer], had an aggressive courtroom

96

demeanor and the personality of a pit bull. In those days, the mob sneered at lawyers with bow ties and fancy diction."

—Eddie Maloney.

"Gotti loved aggressiveness, insisted on it, to hell with subtlety and lawyers being cute."

—Eddie Maloney describing Bruce Cutler.

"I fought tooth and nail for Santo and Jimmy, as I did for every client. It was my obligation as a lawyer to defend even the most unpopular and reprehensible Mafiosi with the maximum zeal I possessed. That was the only way I knew how to practice law."

—Frank Ragano describing his defense of Santo Trafficante and Jimmy Hoffa.

"Don't be bashful. These people can well afford to pay."

—Henry Whitaker, defense lawyer, to fellow lawyer Frank Ragano about fees.

"I'll tell Jimmy the blunt truth. If he wants to hear only good news, he needs a nursemaid, not a lawyer."

—Frank Ragano.

"You can call me Mr. Cutler or Bruce. You don't have to call me 'sir.'"

> —Defense lawyer Bruce Cutler telling Judge Eugene Nickerson to tone down the formality at John Gotti's 1986–1987 trial.

"John, … a majority of these lawyers, who you look at, are known as erudite, professorial, ah, egghead types. Will not put in the brief words to the effect, 'Go fuck yourself!' I know you can't do that. But they will not put into a brief 'and we dispute the existence of the Mafia.' I say it all the time. They won't write it down, they just won't write it down."

> —Bruce Cutler badmouthing his brethren to John Gotti at the Ravenite Social Club.

"Surely his memory is missing or dead."

> —Queens prosecutor Kirke Bartley, after a judge ruled Bartley could not use the grand jury testimony of Romual Piecyk—who had testified in a grand jury that John Gotti had beaten him but was terrified to say it in court—as evidence at Gotti's trial because Piecyk was neither missing or dead.

"We'd love to bring you witnesses with absolutely impeccable credentials, of unquestionable honesty and integrity. The problem is, they don't know any such people."

> —Federal prosecutor Gleeson, explaining to jurors why 19-time killer Salvatore "Sammy Bull" Gravano was a primary witness against Gotti and codefendant Frank Locascio.

"Jack Cicillini ... He's a lawyer .... Not much of a lawyer. Like you."

> —John Gotti, telling lawyer Bruce Cutler that Gotti and leaders of the New England family are going to communicate through their lawyers.

"Gambino Crime Family? This is the Shargel, Cutler, and whattaya call it Crime Family."

> —John Gotti complaining about his lawyers' fees.

"They all want their money up front. You get four guys that want sixty five, seventy five thousand a piece, up front. You're talking about three hundred thousand in one month! Cocksuckers!"

> —Gotti again, on lawyers' fees.

"When Johnny (Carneglia) told me what he gave these fucking guys, in two and a half years, gave 'em a fuckin' mill …. The indictment should read, then, 'John Carneglia and Lawyer!' He's your fuckin' partner. And he's the senior partner."

—Gotti, one more time,
on lawyers' fees.

"After they pass the bar, every lawyer should have to spend six months in jail, just so they know what it's like."

—Late Gambino capo Joe
Butch Corrao on lawyers.

"They're overpriced, overpaid, and, and underper-formed … And they ain't got the balls to do what they're supposed to do."

—Gotti's consigliere Frank
Locascio on lawyers.

"They got a routine now, the two lawyers. 'Muck' and 'Fuck' I call them. When I see Bruce, 'Hi, Jerry loves you,' he says. 'He's in your corner one hundred per-cent.' When I see Jerry, 'Hi, Bruce loves you. He's in your corner a hundred percent.' 'I know youse both love me!'"

—John Gotti about Bruce Cutler
and Gerald Shargel, the lawyers
who won his 1990 acquittal
on assault charges.

"I think the government will stop at nothing to create a case against Alphonse Persico. The search warrant was a pretext to harass him. They stayed in the house for 16 hours, tearing the place up and down, and they came up with a lot of nothing. They just put away Gotti's son, now they want to put away [Carmine] Persico's son."

—Lawyer Barry Levin attempting to convince a federal judge that the FBI lacked the required probable cause to search the apartment of Carmine Persico's 21-year-old granddaughter in an effort to look for evidence against her father Alphonse.

"He don't know why, he don't know who, and he don't know what."

—Defense lawyer Joe Santaguida to detectives about his client, Michael Ciancaglini.

"My client ... never was nor is he presently a member of any organized crime family. He is a hardworking individual who through sheer individual effort has achieved a degree of success in the solid waste business ... It's an American success story, not an organized crime story."

—Carmine Franco's criminal defense attorney.

"Schultz is not a Dillinger. He is not a Baby Face Nelson. He is indicted for failure to pay income taxes. Is this a serious crime to man?"

—J. Richard Davis,
Dutch Schultz's lawyer.

"This was a major league, major league case. I want to get in the game, you know. That's the athlete part of me coming out—if this is the biggest game in town, then I want to be in it."

—Anthony Cardinale on becoming the lead attorney representing Gennaro Angiulo in the biggest organized crime case in Boston's history.

Leisure Time

"He was pretty well weather beaten. When I saw him, I saw that the band, the official band on his leg and I knew that belonged to Great Britain or England. The bird was in a race in France and hit bad weather and wound up at Staten Island, at my coop, and he's become a celebrity since then."

—Genovese soldier Joseph Ida, on how he rescued a British racing pigeon who made a wrong turn at the English Channel and ended up in his pigeon coop on Staten Island.

"I don't know no doctors or lawyers. Who am I supposed to hang out with? Send me to jail. Send me to jail. I can talk to all my friends in jail."

—Gambino soldier Michael "Mikey Gal" Guerrieri, when told he couldn't associate with wiseguys if he were granted bail.

"You want to know something Mikey? I noticed that on Monday morning … and Thursday morning, I noticed, that people drive all fucked up. It's all the kids coming home from Brooklyn that live in Long Island that are drinking and fuckin' partying."

—Colombo associate Frank "Frank Campy" Campanella bitching about the problems of our times.

"I spent thousands partying, with the guys and with beautiful women, gambling at the track, buying expensive clothes. 'Make it fast, it never lasts' many wiseguys say."

—Eddie Maloney.

"Frank, you've got to remember, over here there's something for everybody. You want opera, they have opera. You want baseball, they have baseball. You want ballroom dancing, they have ballroom dancing. And if you want sex shows, they have live sex shows. That's what makes this place so great."

—Santo Trafficante about Cuba.

"After that, the boys double-checked to make sure the safety catch was on before they deposited any gun in a golf bag."

—Caddy Tim Sullivan, explaining a change in procedure after Al Capone's revolver went off in his golf bag, shooting him in the leg.

"Throughout my career, I was to find that the most rabid fans in the fight business were the gangsters on one hand, and the society crowd on the other. And whenever they met at parties honoring this champ or that one, they got along like brothers under the skin. However, the society people sometimes got drunk and nasty, but the gangsters were always gentlemen."

—Chicago boxer Barney Ross on gangsters as boxing fans.

"I go to the movies in the daytime because this way when I come out at night, I don't have to worry about being followed."

—Colombo consigliere Vinnie Aloi on why he goes to the movies in the late afternoon.

"Turn off them fucking soap boxes! You should be out stealing and looking for business."

—Lefty Guns Ruggiero when he caught crew members watching soap operas.

"After all, I like baseball. Because I happen to have some income tax trouble doesn't mean that I have to bury myself."

—Dutch Schultz.

"My dear, Arthur [Dutch] was the answer to a hostess's prayer. When it became known that he had been invited to your party, you had nothing to worry about. Everyone came … And, really, he was charming. It was hard to believe all those horrid stories."

—A socialite to a *New York Sun* reporter.

"A lot of people have the misconception that mob guys are all big drinkers or dopers. Some of them are—a greater proportion of young guys do drugs than older guys. But so many guys don't do anything that you don't stand out by saying no—it's no big deal. Tony Mirra killed twenty or thirty people, and he drank only club soda."

—FBI Agent Joe "Donnie Brasco" Pistone.

"All I want is a good sandwich. You see this sandwich here? This tuna sandwich? That's all I want, a good sandwich."

—John Gotti.

"Let's take the car."

—What John Gotti would say when he wanted to vacation in Florida.

"Like John Madden and many famous Americans, John does not like to fly."

—Lawyer Bruce Cutler's explanation.

Frank & Fritzy on Vacation

Fritzy: What I had planned to do, as soon as I had gotten a little better, was to go to Florida, just to take a week or two down there, get some …

Frank: Yeah.

Fritzy: … and the water, you know, just some breathin' and that's a good health, you know …

Frank: I'll go with you.

Fritzy: Yeah …

Frank: You go with me you rest.

Fritzy: I rest, I rest alright. I won't rest. With you I will not rest.

Frank: Why?

Fritzy: Nah, you don't wanna go to bed when I go to bed.

Frank: Who?

Fritzy: I'm an early bird. You're like a vampire, you out 'til 5 in the morning.

Frank: You forgot I lived with Fat Dom?

Fritzy: Yeah?

Frank: Who used to go take care of Fat Dom down there? Me. Cut his toenails, lived with 'em.

Fritzy: Whattaya think I'm crippled or something?

Frank: No, I'm just sayin', I was with Fat Dom. I used to go with Fat Dom. I used to sleep and had my own room there and everything.

Fritzy: Yeah?

Love and Marriage

"She had an apron on, she looked like a little house-mother, cooking away, cooking and tasting the sauce and the sausage and the macaroni. She was so different from the sluts that I'm dealing with every other minute at the club .... Then and there I realized that she was for me. And I was right. We would be like wolves who mate, that stay with one another for good. If something should ever happen to one of them, they still don't ever mate again."

—Salvatore "Sammy Bull"
Gravano on his wife.

"I know you are a reporter. And I know what people are saying about my husband .... I'll tell you about him. He's a wonderful man. Thoughtful. Considerate. Our married life has been 12 years of unbroken happiness. He has given me kindness, devotion, love—everything that a good man can give a woman. Look what he did for his mother! Just last year he took her back to her birthplace in Italy. She left there a poor peasant. She came back the richest woman in the village."

—Ann Torrio, wife of Johnny
Torrio, who ran the Chicago
Outfit before Al Capone.

"Another thing, if I had to do it over again, I don't think I would get married. A man is better off without a wife and children. I should never have gotten close to the wives and children of people I do business with, because you come to like their families and when they do something wrong and you have to do something to them, you start worrying about their families."

—Tampa Mafia boss Santo
Trafficante Sr.

"The greatest device ever contrived by mankind to destroy love ... is marriage."

—Frank Sinatra to mob lawyer
Frank Ragano.

"My son's got hot nuts. He can't wait for me to get out of prison to get married. Now, there are a lot of guys who owe me that are friends of yours. I've made a list of names of people to give gifts and I want my son and his girlfriend to have a nice wedding."

—Jimmy Hoffa to mob lawyer
Frank Ragano.

"She was my first steady girl. She was Jewish, but who cared about that? She was pretty, and she had a million-dollar personality. I remember she wore a size twelve, so when we burglarized a dress factory, I always held out a few instead of giving everything to Fats West, the fence."

—Joseph Valachi.

A Cosa Nostra *Romeo and Juliet:* The Courtship of Mildred Reina

By Joseph Valachi

I was amazed when [Mildred's] brother said that it was all right by him [for me] to marry her. But the next thing I hear is that Mildred's in the hospital. She had swallowed a bottle of iodine. I found out why. Her brother told her that I didn't want anything to do with her. So now I know how they work. Her brother says okay to me and tells her just the opposite. Lena [Bobby Doyle's wife] told me not to go up to the house, as there was a big commotion going on there. I told her maybe I better drop the whole thing, but she says, "A fine guy you are. Here she's taken iodine for you, and you're talking this way."

"I look back and I realize that in the end I got everything I dreamed about having when I was still living with my parents in Bensonhurst and longing for escape. I married a handsome man, we became wealthy, we had children, they went to private schools, we lived in a nice big house. So I got everything I always wanted. Some people might say I got everything I deserved. What do they know?"

—Lynda Milito, widow of slain Gambino
soldier Liborio "Louie" Milito.

"So, we got married. Tremendous. It was a hell of a night. Maybe five hundred people. Her family. My family. Friends. Caviar. Lobsters. Cristal champagne for five hundred people. They erected a chapel in Caesar's palace. I have no idea what the bill was. My wedding was comped."

—Frank "Lefty" Rosenthal.

"After a while, when I'd get home, I'd come home very cautiously. Not just because of her pistol, but I was concerned that she would really hire someone."

—Lefty Rosenthal about his wife Geri.

"He started to keep tabs on her like she was a Vegas version of a Stepford wife."

> —A retired FBI agent about Lefty Rosenthal's obsession with his wife.

"But no matter what he did to her, she'd never leave him, because there were always presents. Geri was an old hooker. He bought her when they got married and she stayed bought."

> —A retired FBI agent about the relationship between Frank Rosenthal and his wife Geri.

"He'd [Rosenthal] drive anybody to drink. He'd come home after his show at three or four in the morning, kick her out of bed, and talk to one of his girlfriends on the phone for two hours."

> —Geri's friend Suzanne Kloud.

"He [Rosenthal] gave her a pink coral-and-diamond necklace and she had a cat's-eye necklace surrounded by diamonds. The necklaces were worth two hundred thousand and three hundred thousand dollars. And she lived for that. If you were a hustler, that's your God."

> —Geri's friend Suzanne Kloud.

"She attracted attention wherever she went. She was that much of a knockout. It's one of the problems with marrying a ten, or even a nine. They're dangerous."

—Lefty Rosenthal about his wife Geri.

"I think it was Lefty's generosity with his girlfriends that drove Geri the craziest, not the fact that he had girlfriends."

—Murray Ehrenberg, Lefty Rosenthal's casino manager.

"The most stupid thing I ever did was marry—three times."

—June Lang, ex-wife of Johnny Rosselli.

"I feel like I have much useful advice for women in bad marriages. This I know. You can't make something good when it's bad all the way through."

—Lynda Milito, Mafia widow.

"After all, I was just married a couple of months, and I didn't want Mildred to think I was already starting to fool around."

—Joseph Valachi, explaining why he went home right away after taking part in a mob hit.

"I remember my honeymoon as a wonderful time. In those days, when you traveled 100 miles by car, it was something worth talking about."

—Meyer Lansky on his honeymoon.

"In this life, you can't get married. You're better off if you don't have no fucking body, and this way, that's the end of it."

—John Gotti.

"He was leading a double life with me and a double life with the FBI."

—Theresa Stanley testifying that James "Whitey" Bulger abandoned her for a younger Catherine Greig whom he'd been secretly seeing for 20 years.

"All I know is one thing. I don't think I'll ever find myself in a position where I'll put my wedding money, 380 thousand … whatever it is, in the basement near a broken safe, with a bunch of old jewelry."

—An incredulous John Gotti after learning that the feds had seized what his son Junior said were wedding gifts he had kept in a friend's basement for some seven years.

"Nobody could understand why Vito [Genovese] didn't do anything about her. The word was all around, why don't he hit her? But he must have really cared for her. She had something on him. I remember when we— Vito and me—were in Atlanta together later on, he would sometimes talk about her, and I would see the tears rolling down his cheeks. I couldn't believe it."

—Joseph Valachi discussing the very timid reaction that the volatile Genovese had when wife Anna testified about Vito's racket connections and the size and sources of his income during their divorce proceedings.

"Me and Spike [Anthony DiGregorio, the caretaker of Nicky Scarfo's Florida home] used to be in the house, and we'd hear Nicky giving [his wife] a beating upstairs. Then he'd come down and say, 'Every once in a while you gotta bang 'em around to keep them in line.'"

—Nicholas "The Crow" Caramandi.

"I suppose if I wrote down the pros and cons of the marriage, lots of people might think I was nuts to stay with him, but I guess we all have our own needs, and they're not added up in the columns."

—Karen Hill.

"If you listened, you never heard such woe. One of these hostess parties could have kept a soap opera going for years."

—Karen Hill, describing gatherings
of mob wives she attended.

"They never talked about what their husbands had done to get sent to jail. That just wasn't ever a part of the conversation. What they discussed was how the prosecutors and the cops lied. How people picked on their husbands."

—Karen Hill, describing Mafia wives.

Loyalty

"I'm not here to sit in judgment of Mr. Gotti but in judgment of a friend who betrays a friend. When I was growing up in East Los Angeles, the worst thing was to be a snitch."

—Anthony Quinn on why he came
to watch Salvatore "Sammy Bull"
Gravano testify at Gotti's trial.

"There's a hundred rules. We broke ninety-nine of them. This was the last rule. It wasn't that hard anymore."

—Sammy Bull Gravano on how
he could violate the sacred
Mafia oath of secrecy—*omerta*.

"If you are ordered to kill, you kill. Even your best friend. Even your father. You do it. No question. If you fail, you will be killed. Those who obey will be protected. Those who disobey will be killed."

—Mafia oath.

"I know that they're going to take a shot at me. It could be today, tomorrow, or ten years from now, but it'll come. Instead of being happy that at least one of us made it out, they can't live with it. They'll never leave me alone. I'm not the kind of guy that they'll easily forget."

—Michael "The Yuppie Don" Franzese after he quit the Mob.

Generation Gap

Salvatore "Shotsie" Sparacio: Between you and I, Sal, I think things are a little too loose, too many, taking in too many guys ... I'm saying it's too loose around him [Philadelphia boss John Stanfa].

Salvatore Avena: More than two people?

Sparacio: Shouldn't be.

Avena: If there's more than two people, then you might as well go in the advertising business.

Sparacio: That's right. Shouldn't be. Shouldn't be unless they brag about what they do. These young kids ... Unless you're schooled ten, fifteen, twenty years around somebody, how can you really have faith?

"Take me out of here. I won't talk to these people."

—Lucky Luciano to his jailers when two narcotics agents arrived at the visiting room at the state prison where he was housed after his conviction for running a prostitution ring.

"You go up and mention my name, and in the meantime I will have word out and you will have no difficulties."

—A jailed Lucky Luciano telling Genovese gangster Joe "Socks" Lanza—when Lanza told him during World War II that Naval Intelligence wanted to prevent sabotage on the Brooklyn piers—to go to the Brooklyn docks and mention his name and Luciano would take care of the rest by reaching out to the mob boss of the Brooklyn waterfront, Albert Anastasia.

"I don't know if he's a rat now. Is he gonna be a rat someday? Yeah."

—John Gotti explaining why he wanted the DeCavalcante family to kill soldier Gaetano "Corky" Vastola.

"I was born and raised in This Thing and I'm gonna die in This Thing. But with the right people … Over here, it's like kindergarten."

—John Stanfa, Sicilian-born
Philadelphia mob boss.

"Loyalty. There's not loyalty from the beginning. I never felt so uncomfortable in my … fifty years. Before, you swore with your back up. I watch your back, you watch my back. There was never no problem."

—Shotsie Sparacio, longtime
South Jersey bookmaker.

"Are you crazy, Pat? I don't want to hear this shit. You're my best friend. What are you, kidding? You're my best friend. Without you, I wouldn't be here."

—Nicholas "The Crow" Caramandi,
reassuring Pat Spirito after Nicholas got
an order to take part in Pat's execution.

Loyalty

"I finally decided to cooperate against her family [when] I learned that she secretly recorded me on tape for the mob. The same day when I learned of the tapes, [that] she taped me for Bones, that's when I decided to come clean about her family. That's the first time I ever spoke to them about her Uncle Tony, her brother Frank Smith, her father, her cousin Michael and her cousin Vincent. I felt that she had crossed the line. If you want to go out with somebody else, you don't want to wait for me, that's one thing. If you want to hold my son from me—maybe later on you'll see the reasons why I'm doing these things and maybe you'll settle down and maybe I will get a chance to see my kid. But once you want to go against me and you want to go with the people that tried to kill my father and abuse my family, you want to sign in with the mob, then … I can't trust you any more."

—Turncoat Luchese soldier Frank Gioia Jr. explaining why after withholding all criminal information against girlfriend Kim Smith's family for two years, he implicated them in all the crimes he knew they committed.

The Media

"I got a plan to get the press off of John's [John Gotti's] back, a diversion to get the heat off. We can kill Oliver North. You know, that soldier that caused all that trouble down in Washington. If we kill him, there'll be so much attention over that, the public, the news media, won't pay no attention to John anymore."

—Joe Piney Armone.

"I have been the subject of one of the most malicious characterizations based upon utter falsehood, devious innuendos and criminal-sounding inferences for no other reason than news sensationalism."

—Mob-connected Las Vegas
casino operator, Allen
Glick, talking to reporters.

"Well, my name is Whitey Bulger, motherfucker, and I kill people for a living."

—James "Whitey" Bulger
to Paul Corsetti, a *Boston
Herald* crime reporter.

"In the Mafia, it was all about money. These so-called experts on 'the mob' never seemed to understand this, which is one reason I didn't pay attention to what they wrote in the papers."

—Lynda Milito, Mafia wife.

"How come you keep writing all those bad things about my brother Albert? He ain't killed nobody in your family ... yet."

—Anthony Anastasio complaining
to a newspaper reporter about his
coverage of his brother Albert.

"I'm only talkin' about what I know ... What I seen with my own eyes. And what I done. Not what they write in books or what you see in movies. That's all bullshit. That's rats and agents talking."

—Joseph "Hoboken Joe" Stassi.

"I'll only make an official statement when I'm actually killed."

—Ohio Congressman James
Traficant to reporters.

"I always treat you like a gentleman, John. This is no good."

> —John Gotti, to reporter John Miller, after Miller and a camera crew ambushed Gotti outside his Little Italy social club.

"Good, the people like me."

> —John Gotti, to reporters who asked about his chances at trial.

"Don't you read the papers?"

> —Simone "Sam the Plumber" DeCavalcante, a few days after the U.S. Attorney's office released transcripts of hundreds of FBI wiretaps of the Mafia chieftain and an attendant at a Newark, NJ parking lot asked him, "What's new?"

"I'm not lily white, but most of the stuff the newspapers reported about me was the bunk and they knew it."

> —Al Capone.

Do as I Say, Not as I Do

Al Capone, answering a few questions about newspapermen.

Q. What do you think of newspapermen who turn their profession into a racket?

A. Newspapers and newspapermen should be busy suppressing rackets and not supporting them. It does not become me of all persons to say that, but I believe it.

Q. How many newspapermen have you had on your payroll?

A. Plenty.

"The papers say I'm Public Enemy Number 6. I should get a better spot. I'm working hard on it."

—Bugsy Siegel.

"You guys sure are good at walking backwards."

—Meyer Lansky, to photographers
and reporters as they retreated
in front of him.

"I don't want to spoil the 'drammer' of your stories. So I don't think I'll say anything."

—Meyer Lansky, to reporters after
an appearance before a grand jury.

"I got absolutely nothing to say, nothing. What do I need interviews for? What do I need it for? Nobody's gonna write anything good about me."

> —Meyer Lansky, whipping
> out a one-liner to reporters
> on another occasion.

"I think that you ought to pay me half the money that you've made writing about me."

> —Meyer Lansky to author
> Hank Messick.

"Now, why couldn't you have made me more sympathetic? After all, I am a grandfather."

> —Meyer Lansky to Lee Strasberg
> who portrayed a character based
> on Lansky in *Godfather Part II*.

"I don't try to fool or impose on nobody. If I just met you casually, I would call myself a restaurant operator. If we warmed up to each other, I would tell you I was a common gambler. I don't sail under no false colors."

> —Meyer Lansky on how he would
> describe his livelihood.

"I never met a real honest-to-god gangster."

> —Mario Puzo, at the time the
> movie *The Godfather* was released.

"These gang movies are making a lot of kids want to be tough guys, and they don't serve any useful purpose. Why, they ought to take all of them and throw them in the lake. They're doing nothing but harm to the younger element ..."

> —Al Capone, on gangster movies.

"They want a full show, all the courtroom trappings, the hue and cry, and all the rest. It's utterly impossible for a man of my age to have done all the things with which I'm charged. I'm a spook, born of a million minds."

> —Al Capone on the way he had
> been portrayed by the media.

"When Sammy Bull Gravano walked into federal court and confronted John Gotti, it was the most electric courtroom moment I ever felt. Ten years later, it still is."

> —Courtroom sketch
> artist Ruth Pollack.

"My orbs had caught sight of the largest automatic I ever saw ... He covered the gun with one of his immense paws and hid it on the other side of the table .... 'I don't understand that,' I said, 'Here you are playing a game of cards with your friends, but you keep a gun handy' ... 'I have no friends,' he said as he handed me a glass of grand beer."

—Legendary newsman Walter
Winchell on talking to Al Capone.

"I suppose there ain't no wars around, so they have to put me on the front page."

—Dutch Schultz on his appearance
at a local ballgame.

"Get the fuck away from me."

—Seventy-five-year-old Gambino
capo James "Jimmy Brown" Failla,
swinging his cane at Pablo Guzman
as the TV reporter asked him
about murder charges that had
been filed against him.

"That is beside the pernt. I only remember it made me feel bad when I saw it in the *[New York] Times*. I don't think 'pushover for a blonde' is any kind of language to write for a newspaper like the *Times*."

—Dutch Schultz's rctort to a *Times*
reporter who wrote that Dutch
was a pushover for a blonde.

"I haven't been hiding. I've just been busy, busy, all the time busy."

> —Anthony DeTolve, Sam "Momo" Giancana's nephew, during a press interview. To the media he became "Busy-Busy" DeTolve, which doomed his candidacy for alderman.

"I was not released from prison because of any special services rendered to the United States in the past war, but only because American courts recognized my full innocence."

> —Lucky Luciano lying to United Press International about why he was released, most likely so Italian Mafiosi wouldn't think he was an informer.

"I got my pardon because of the great services I rendered the United States and because, after all, they reckoned I was innocent."

> —Lucky Luciano putting a little different spin in this comment to the Associated Press, perhaps in an effort to pave the way for a return to the United States.

"You newspaper birds are to blame [for my troubles] but I don't hold it against you. I was a little shaky when I read some of your stuff but when that jury disagreed I knew you couldn't fool the people too much. You've made me Public Enemy No. 1 and the jury didn't believe it."

—Dutch Schultz after his trial
ended in a hung jury.

"Don't forget, when you write your piece, to split all my infinitives for me."

—Dutch Schultz to Walter Lister,
the *New York Post*'s city editor.

Money

"My wife, children and I have endured these types of false accusations since 1990, none of which are true or have merit. The source of any monies recovered has already been explained to the authorities."

—John A. "Junior" Gotti explaining
away a $350,000 cache of cash that
ultimately led to him pleading
guilty to racketeering charges.

"One time he went to the jewelry shop. Just like we'd go in and buy yogurt. He bought a hundred-thousand-dollar jewel for some girl. When he took out a credit card to pay for it, the poor clerk saw her sale evaporating. But when she checked his Visa card, it turned out that he had a one-million-dollar credit line."

—Frank "Lefty" Rosenthal talking
about Adnan Khashoggi.

"Everything's nice and cool. There's money pouring in like there's no tomorrow. I've never seen so much money."

—Johnny Rosselli in 1960 at the
pinnacle of his criminal career.

"Everyone loves cash. It makes them smile."

—Liborio "Louie" Milito.

"These people always pay in cash; it's legal tender. They don't keep checking accounts and records of how much money they have."

—Henry Whitaker, defense lawyer,
to Frank Ragano about fees.

"With the money we're making, we don't need anything. We don't need this car. We don't need this arm rest! We don't need this sun visor! We don't need nothing, Michael! I can just buy another new Cadillac tomorrow."

—Lawrence "Fat Larry" Iorizzo to
Michael "The Yuppie Don"
Franzese, while stripping the
inside of his car, piece by piece.

"Sure I got a racket. So's everybody. Name me a guy that ain't got a racket. Most guys hurt people. I don't hurt nobody. Only them that get in my way. I give away a lot of dough. Maybe I don't support no college or build no libraries, but I give it to people that need it, direct."

—Al Capone.

Money

"That means $1 million every two months was being paid to just one racketeer .... It's a big business, run by big business methods. Schultz's accounts were obviously kept by an expert accountant. The entries were in perfect order, just like the books of a big corporation. And Schultz, who was notoriously close-fisted, knew where every penny went, even to buying the morning papers."

—The FBI's J. Edgar Hoover.

"I ain't admitting anything but the record will show that I tried to pay my income tax and the government refused to touch it. Sure I got dough. I'd be a sucker if I didn't have some."

—Dutch Schultz.

"A thousand dollars, what would I do with a thousand dollars? I give that to broken-down old broads."

—Murray "Hump" Humphrey when offered $1,000 a month in return on an investment.

"I guess the public could say mob guys were racist because they just strictly deal with Italians. But I think they're the most unracist people in the world. They're just greedy. The only color they care about is green, the color of money."

—Salvatore "Sammy Bull" Gravano.

"Sometimes wiseguys can be just as cheap as anybody else, so if they get a free phone, they use them. Essentially, what the cooperator did was, he purported to have contacts where he could get free phone service and he volunteered the phones."

—Assistant U.S. Attorney Maria Barton explaining how the FBI used an undercover operative to supply wiretapped cell phones to greedy New Jersey mobsters.

"For the older guys, the Mafia was a way of life. For these younger guys, it's a way to make money."

—Fred Martens, former executive director of the Pennsylvania Crime Commission.

The Good Life?

John Gotti's trial lawyer and Gotti's former underboss going back and forth at Gotti's racketeering and murder trial.

Albert Krieger: You went from a man who may have lived humbly in the '60s, an environment of which you spoke, to a home in Staten Island and probably had an excess of a million dollars put into it, correct?

Sammy Bull Gravano: That, you're not correct on. That, you're not correct on.

Krieger: Less than a million dollars?

Gravano: A lot less.

Krieger: A lot less. You lived humbly and simply?

Gravano: I guess.

Krieger: You guess?

Gravano: Yeah.

Krieger: Tell us. You should know your own lifestyle, sir. You should know whether you're living well or you're not living well.

Gravano: I'm living well.

Krieger: Pardon?

Gravano: I said I'm living well.

Krieger: Now?

Gravano: Not right this minute.

Murder

"Make him go away."

> —Chicago Outfit boss Paul "The Waiter" Ricca, ordering a murder.

"Johnny did a lot of work when he was a kid. He did a lot of fuckin' work [murder], don't worry."

> —Aladena "Jimmy the Weasel" Fratianno, Johnny Rosselli's friend and occasional hit man.

"If a guy's a rat, sure, then it's honorable."

> —Salvatore Profaci on a time and place for murder.

"Louie Di Bono. And I sat with this guy. I saw the papers and everything. He didn't rob nothin'. You know why he's dying? He's gonna die because he refused to come in when I called. He didn't do nothing else wrong."

> —John Gotti.

Murder

"It was dumb, but that was the way we did things. Whack 'em first and worry about them later."

—Henry Hill.

"If you're part of a crew, nobody ever tells you that they're going to kill you. It doesn't happen that way. There aren't any great arguments or finger-biting curses like in Mafia movies. Your murderers come with smiles. They come as friends, people who have cared deeply about you all your life, and they always come at a time when you are at your weakest and most in need of their help and support."

—Henry Hill.

"Murder was the only way everybody stayed in line. It was the ultimate weapon. Nobody was immune. You got out of line, you got whacked. Everyone knew the rules, but still people got out of line and people kept getting whacked."

—Henry Hill.

"[Jimmy "The Gent" Burke and Tommy Stabile] buried Remo in the backyard at Robert's, under a layer of cement right next to the bocce court. From then on, every time they played, Jimmy and Tommy used to say, 'Hi Remo, how ya doing?'"

—Henry Hill.

"Shooting people was a normal thing for them. It was no big deal. You didn't have to do anything. You just had to be there."

—Henry Hill.

"Only Capone kills like that."

—Bugs Moran.

"The only man who kills like that is Bugs Moran."

—Al Capone.

"We took this guy—this guy was a stool pigeon for the agents. They had a twenty-four-hour guard on him. Plus, where he went, they had the joint surrounded. And we took him right from the middle! Took him with a wheelbarrow! Never heard a thing like that, huh? Ray [De Carlo] knows a little bit of that story. Took him right out of the middle! Took the guy's car and everything!"

—Bayonne Joe Zicarelli,
describing a murder.

"The reason I don't want to kill him is we can't be killing each other every day."

—Nicodemo "Little Nicky" Scarfo.

Murder

"I wish that motherfucker was alive, so I could kill him again."

—Salvie Testa.

"If I could bring the motherfucker back to life, I'd kill him again."

—Philadelphia underboss Philip Leonetti about Vincent Falcone.

"You know, sometimes I lose my temper, and I say, 'Gee I wish somebody would bump that guy off,' and then one of these young punks who wants to make a name for himself goes ahead and does it. And then I have to pick up the pieces."

—Al Capone.

"Go ahead, I want him dead. Yeah, I feel sad. But that's what he gets for being dumb."

—John Gotti.

"No witness ever lived to testify against me."

—Milwaukee boss Frank Balistrieri.

Wanted: A Bulletproof Plastic Bag

Defense Lawyer Ephraim Savitt: You told us that you had a plastic bag over the gun in order to collect the shells?

Dino Basciano: Yes.

Savitt: So you had the gun in a plastic bag?

Basciano: Yes.

Savitt: When you were shooting Patricia Capozzalo?

Basciano: Yes.

Savitt: Is that correct?

Basciano: Yes.

Savitt: But somehow this plastic bag, I guess, it must have blown off when you shot?

Basciano: It made a hole in the front.

Savitt: Was it your idea to put a plastic bag over the gun to collect shells?

Basciano: I don't know whose idea it was.

Savitt: But it didn't work?

Basciano: The shells fell out through the hole.

Murder

"Right over there [in the East River], that's where we dump the bodies. One time some wiseguys dumped two bodies in there. Couple cops from the Seventh Precinct happened to see the bodies dumped. They didn't want to be bothered with it. So they took their little boat out and dragged the bodies down the river to the next precinct so they wouldn't have to investigate the case.

—Lefty Guns Ruggiero.

"Just take me with you, I'm a capable guy. I've done some work. ... Years ago, me and Vinny, we killed a cop."

—Tony Francesehi trying to convince Luchese soldier Frank Gioia Jr. that his help would be useful in a murder plot that Gioia was involved in.

"It was as simple and undramatic as that ... just one quick motion of the hand. The Dutchman did that murder just as casually as if he were picking his teeth."

—Lawyer J. Richard "Dixie" Davis describing how Dutch murdered Jules Martin.

"When DeeBee got whacked, they told me a story. I was in jail when I whacked him. I knew why it was being done. I done it, anyway. I allowed it to be done."

—John Gotti, admitting ordering the murder of Robert DiBernardo.

"We respect your efforts on his behalf. However, the crime he committed is unforgivable. The guy's got to go. That's the end of it."

—Colombo boss Carmine "Junior" Persico meting out the ultimate penalty.

Nicknames

"Between ourselves we'll call him Marteduzzo."

> —Santo Trafficante in response to
> Frank Ragano who explained his
> nickname for Jimmy Hoffa—
> Marteduzzo (Little Hammer)
> because Jimmy pounded away at
> everyone almost continuously.

"The big man on 116th Street was Ciro Terranova, the Artichoke King. He got the name because he tied up all the artichokes in the city. The way I understand it he would buy all the artichokes that came into New York. I didn't know where they all came from, but I know he was buying them all out. Being artichokes, they hold; they can keep. Then Ciro would make his own price and as you know, Italians got to have artichokes to eat."

> —Joseph Valachi.

"Right after this I was mopping up one day in the dormitory with Dolly Dimples. His real name was Carmine Clementi, but he was known as Dolly Dimples because he was a handsome kid with blue eyes and light-brown hair. There were two singers in those days called the Dolly Sisters who were very big, and everyone at Sing Sing [Prison] used to call us the Dolly Sisters because we went around together all the time."

—Joseph Valachi.

A Shrewd Bird by Another Name

Defense Attorney: Why or how did you get the nickname "Crow"?

Nicholas "The Crow" Caramandi: It means shrewd bird.

Attorney: Who gave you that name?

Caramandi: A fella from the neighborhood.

Attorney: He must have known you pretty good.

Caramandi: Probably.

Nicknames

"Yeah, but, either you gotta be proud of who you are, and fight for it, or you gotta be ashamed of it and do like some other lowlifes do, and change their names .... I mean if you ask a guy next door, 'Hey what do you think about the Agnellos?' He'd say, 'Who are the Agnellos?' ... You should stay off television. You should stay off the book covers. You should use Victoria Agnello, and they won't know who the kids are and they won't be faced with this problem. Am I correct or incorrect?"

—John Gotti to daughter
Victoria Gotti-Agnello.

"Jimmy got his nickname, 'Jimmy the Gent' because he used to take the driver's license [when he hijacked a truck], just like everyone else, except Jimmy used to stuff a fifty-dollar bill into the guy's wallet before taking off."

—Henry Hill.

"Never put your name on anything!"

—Paul Vario.

"I was dealing drugs with Georgie Goggles and then Georgie Goggles went on the lam and he referred me to deal with his under guy, who was another—a made guy named Jimmy Froggy, Jimmy Galione. I call him Froggy."

—Dino Basciano.

"Now I know this guy Jimmy Brassiere. He used to bring in shipments of women's clothes from overseas and sell them to department stores. One time he got a huge load of brassieres. That's how he got his name. "

—Salvatore "Sammy Bull" Gravano.

"I found an empty store in a real shopping area on 86th Street. It was a tiny store. I named it 'The Hole in the Wall.' As I was a crook, we called ourselves 'The Hole in the Wall Gang.' Jimmy Brassiere supplied us."

—Sammy Bull Gravano.

"If he had a gun, he'd have to take it apart and put it back together. He'd take the bullets out and then put them back in. Always playing. Always touching … Philip used to worry about fingerprints cause Twitch hadda touch everything, all the bullets, all the pieces of the gun."

—Brenda Colletti explaining why she and her husband Philip nick-named Salvatore Brunetti "Twitch."

146

"The Teflon is gone. The Don is covered with Velcro."

—New York FBI boss Jim Fox uses
the media's favorite nickname for
Gotti to bask in his conviction.

How Ronald Moran Became Messy Marvin

Federal Prosecutor Stephen Kelly: Sir, when you were on the streets did you know a person by the name of Messy Marvin?

Dino Basciano: Yes.

Kelly: Do you know his true name?

Basciano: No. I only know him as Marvin.

Judge Raymond Dearie: Did you say "Messy"?

Basciano: Yes. Called him Messy Marvin.

Kelly: And that's how you knew him on the street?

Basciano: Yes. He looked like the kid from the commercial Messy Marvin.

Kelly: Can you describe his physical appearance?

Basciano: Glasses. He looked—just looked like the kid that played Messy Marvin on TV.

Odds and Ends

"Be careful. And make sure you introduce yourself to Joe Butter so he knows you were there."

> —Victor "Little Vic" Orena giving final instructions to his son about attending the demonstration outside the courthouse for John Gotti's sentencing.

"Southie's safe because it's so fuckin' dangerous."

> —Lifelong resident of South Boston.

"He's got to worry. If he gets pinched, all them years he spent in that fucking asylum (would be) for nothing."

> —Anthony "Fat Tony" Salerno on Vincent "Chin" Gigante's longtime crazy act.

"People mistake my kindness for weakness."

> —Gambino soldier Liborio "Louie" Milito.

Odds and Ends

"Like Louie, I was always kind of suspicious."

—Lynda Milito, Mafia wife.

"Frank, my strength lies in the fact that any member who has a dime can talk to me."

—Jimmy Hoffa explaining to
lawyer Frank Ragano why he
answered every call.

"At Christmas, Tuddy taught me how to drill holes in the trunks of junk Christmas trees he's get for nothing, and then I'd stuff the holes with loose branches. I'd stuff so many branches that even those miserable spindly trees looked full. Then we'd sell them for premium prices, usually at night and mostly around the Euclid Avenue subway stop. It took a day or two before the branches came loose and began to fall apart. The trees would collapse even faster once they were weighed down with decorations."

—Henry Hill.

"Once you get pinched for Shylocking, you get pinched for extortion, money laundering, and then the IRS comes in to break your balls."

—Colombo soldier Anthony
Stropoli describing a recent turn
for the worse for him.

"I take credit for my, my, my bad doings. I made mistakes."

—John Gotti.

"Some friends invited me. I shouldn't have gone."

—Santo Trafficante commenting
on the Apalachian meeting.

"… let me tell you about Paul, Sammy. He didn't—he was a fucking fish on the desert. He was a fish outta water. He don't know this life!"

—John Gotti telling Salvatore "Sammy Bull"
Gravano how he feels about Paul Castellano.

Sammy Bull Gravano as Beauty School Dropout

"I'm getting laid every three minutes. In closets, on massage tables, every time I turn around, practically. What I'm supposed to be learning is haircutting. And I am the worst, the absolute and total world's worst. One day I'm doing a haircut on some lady. She had straight hair, nothing fancy, so it's fairly easy. Just even everything out, shoulder length. She's sitting in the chair chatting away and I'm talking to her. All of a sudden, she ain't saying nothing. I feel like I'm talking to the wall. I look down at her and there's a wire hanging on her chest. I'm thinking, what the fuck is that? I said, 'Sweetheart, I'm talking to you. Are you deaf?' She turns around and says, 'What?' That's when I saw it. She has a hearing aid and I cut the wire to it. Unfucking believable!"

"They ain't like in New York, they say hello; to tell the truth it caught me off balance until I got used to it."

—Joseph Valachi, on people
in Connecticut.

"I hope the American people will benefit by knowing what the mob is like. If I was killed in Atlanta [in prison], I would have died branded as a rat anyway without doing anything wrong. So what did I lose [by revealing what I knew]?"

—Joseph Valachi, on how his deci-
sion to break his vow of silence and
tell all he knew about the Mafia
would affect the American people.

"If I had to give a mark, a grade on how every situation was handled—the lawyers and everything else, jobs and getting jobs and working and all that—I can't put a passing mark on one incident."

—John Gotti grades son Junior on
his reign as acting boss.

"I fixed it. I was in charge of a guy on the jury. Did a good job, didn't I?"

—Sammy Bull Gravano talking to
FBI agents about Gotti's acquittal
in his first racketeering trial.

"Paulie [Vario] and Johnny Dio used to push me to go [back] to school. They wanted me to become an ophthalmologist. I don't know why but that's what they wanted me to be."

—Henry Hill.

"Jimmy [Burke] was the kind of guy who cheered for the crooks in movies."

—Henry Hill on one of his former pals.

"Paulie was smiling. It was like he was proud. He made a big thing out of the presentation. He didn't usually do such things, so everybody showed up. He had a box all wrapped up and made me open it in front of all the guys. They were real quiet. I took off the paper, and inside was one of those wide-angle, rearview mirrors that truck drivers use to be able to see everybody coming up behind them. The mirror was about three feet long. 'Put it in the car,' Paulie said. 'It'll help you make tails.'"

—Henry Hill, on a gift he got from his mob mentor, Luchese capo Paul Vario.

"I just don't like to fly, so I used to drink before we got on the plane. One time I got so drunk they wouldn't let me on. I hadda wait till the next flight."

—Nicholas "The Crow" Caramandi,
on his fear of flying.

"When I started an office, I had people working in there who had nothing to do with the work. Anybody caught with a black pencil gets fired. They don't have to do nothing, just have a black pencil. The only thing they are allowed to have are red or blue pencils. You understand?"

—Angelo Bruno on how he
stopped people from altering
bookmaking records.

"One man … kept coming to the front and arguing and so forth. And he got hit in the head with a mallet, and Jimmy Hoffa said, 'Sergeant of arms, please remove this object from the floor so we can continue the meeting.' The sergeant of arms come and got him, took him outside. About 20 minutes he was back in, and I have to say he acted like a gentleman when he came back in."

—Former Teamsters Union
President Roy Williams describing
how Jimmy Hoffa maintained order
at a union meeting.

"Cause now it's Saint Valentine's Day. That's when all them guys got killed in Chicago. I don't want no Valentine's Day massacre here."

—Colombo capo Gregory Scarpa
on why he called off a heist.

"The minute I walked out the door they pulled right up on me. It happened I had the receipts of the [illegal bets] still in my hand. They asked for my identification and I … said, 'I'll go in the house and get it.' They said never mind, just get in the car. I said, 'Am I under arrest?' and they just said get in the car. So they took me to the 102nd Precinct in Queens. So I asked them up there if I could go to the bathroom, claiming I was sick. So they went in with me, and picked the one with no toilet paper, and then I asked them for some toilet paper. The guy said I'll get you some, so I quickly stuffed the receipts in the john and flushed it. The cop asked me why I did that. I said because of the stink."

—Gaetano "Corky" Vastola
telling Simone "Sam the
Plumber" DeCavalcante
how he beat the cops.

"If I were the director of a *Godfather* movie, I would be happy to find someone who looks just like him .... I am a bit puzzled, however, why men like him in your country always seem to have the best lawyers."

—Vladimir P. Dounaey, chief correspondent of Soviet television and radio talking about Gotti during his 1992 racketeering trial.

"What am I, Santa Claus?"

—Peter Zuccaro, an armored-car robber, testifying that he did not give anything from his $1 million haul to anyone in the Gotti crowd.

"This is pathetic. I don't even get ice cream out of it. I love those fuckin' frozen red somethin's. We got the company three years, never saw a dime. Never seen an ice cream bar out of it! If you took [the money] and you put it on the street for a point and a half, we'd be rich over three years! We be rich without all the ice cream meltin' or nothin'."

—John Gotti, complaining about a bad investment in an ice cream company.

"I didn't want them to see me laughing."

> —Bookmaker Frank Erickson
> explaining later why he dropped his
> head in apparent contrition when
> he told a Senate hearing that his
> illegal activities made him feel
> unworthy of being an American.

"Like a ballplayer, that's me. I figure I get seasoning doing these jobs here. Somebody from one of the big mobs spots me. Then, up to the big leagues."

> —Harry Straus a.k.a. Pittsburgh
> Phil a.k.a. Big Harry a.k.a. Pep on
> working your way up.

"It's pretty tough when a citizen with an unblemished record must be hounded from his home by the very policemen whose salaries are paid, at least in part, from the victim's pocket. You might say that every policeman in Chicago gets some of his bread and butter from the taxes I pay."

> —Al Capone.

"That was it. No more letters from truant officers. No more letters from the school. In fact, no more letters from anybody. Finally, after a couple of weeks, my mother had to go down to the post office and complain."

—Henry Hill, after mob friends
assaulted and threatened his mail-
man not to deliver truancy letters
from school to Henry's house.

"That's a *lake?* That looks like a fucking ocean. Look at the boats out there! Ships! ... You sure it's not the ocean and they just call it something else? Unfucking-believable."

—An incredulous Lefty Guns
Ruggiero, when told that the huge
body of water he was looking at was
not the ocean, but Lake Michigan.

"Artie, Hy and I were just kids from the Jewish ghetto running a record company that exploded into a hundred-million-dollar operation before we learned what the hell we were doing. Sonny kept the wolves away. He never asked for anything in return. I love the guy."

—Phil Steinberg, young record producer,
befriended by John "Sonny" Franzese.

"We're gonna wind up in the joint here—me, I know, definitely."

> —DeCavalcante soldier Gaetano "Corky" Vastola, accurately predicting the future for himself and Roulette Records President Morris Levy regarding their shady record deals.

"A frame can be a lot worse than something you actually done because you don't know what they're gonna throw against you."

> —Sammy Bull Gravano.

"I'm from South Boston. We keep things to ourselves."

> —A witness after recanting his testimony in an organized crime case.

"How do you hide a five-hundred-pound man in a Hawaiian shirt?"

> —Prosecutor talking about the difficulty of placing Lawrence "Fat Larry" Iorizzo in the Federal Witness Protection Program.

"Believe me ... you know, I just go by what I hear, from one lawyer to another lawyer. They ... they no have a real full dish of spaghetti."

> —John Stanfa offering his assessment of a government probe.

Odds and Ends

"I want to settle down and be a plain citizen and be given a chance to earn a living. I want to be plain Arthur Flegenheimer and forget there ever was a Dutch Schultz. That bird has had too much trouble."

—Dutch Schultz.

"I never found any place as good as New York. I never used to go away on vacations. I never went to Florida—though they gave a couple of cops a swell vacation, sending them down to Miami to look for me."

—Dutch Schultz.

"Anita! Children! These two gentlemen are FBI agents. They have come out here to accuse me of killing Arthur Adler! I cry out to God up above! If I am guilty to killing Arthur Adler may God come down, right now, and put cancer in the eyeballs—of you, and you, and you!"

—Sam "Mad Sam" DeStefano march-
ing in front of his family and their
friends as he pointed his finger at the
two men who showed up at his house.

"I guess I'm gonna need all the luck I can get, so I ain't passing anything up."

—Dutch Schultz on accepting
rosary beads from one well-wisher
and a murmured "Good luck"
in Yiddish from another.

Sometimes, There *Is* Such a Thing as a Free Lunch!

Defense Lawyer Ephraim Savitt: Did you ever tie up a driver and, you know, sort of kidnap the driver for a while during a course of a truck hijacking?

Dino Basciano: Yeah. We took a guy out to lunch one time.

Savitt: Out to where?

Basciano: Took him to lunch.

Savitt: A lunch?

Basciano: We took him to a diner. He hung out with us until the load got dropped and then we dropped him off.

Savitt: Never tied up the driver?

Basciano: Nope. We left him at a beach, left him on a corner. Never tied him up. They stood with us in—either in the car or a van.

Savitt: The worst you ever did to a driver was take him to a diner and buy him lunch?

Basciano: That was the best we ever did to a driver.

Savitt: What is the worst you ever did to a driver?

Basciano: Not give him lunch.

"Prohibition was the greatest curse the country ever saw. For the first time it changed the saying that crime doesn't pay."

—Charles B. McLaughlin, District
Attorney of the Bronx.

"All I ever did was to sell beer and whiskey to our best people."

—Al Capone.

"I never did anything to deserve that reputation [Public Enemy No. 1], unless it was to supply good beer to people who wanted it."

—Dutch Schultz.

Philosophizing

"It's better to live one day as a lion than a hundred years as a lamb."

—Bruce Cutler describing
John Gotti's credo.

"Some people look back at their lives and wonder how and why it turned out the way it did. I don't wonder about mine. They say that life is what you make it. I'm sorry, but to me that's not how it works. Life is what happens to you and how you deal with it."

—Lynda Milito, Mafia wife.

"When Christ died on the cross, the closest man to him was a thief, and that's good enough for me."

—Chicago Outfit mobster
Johnny Rosselli.

"I don't try to fool or impose on nobody. If I just met you casually, I would call myself a restaurant operator. If we warmed up to each other, I would tell you I was a common gambler. I don't sail under no false colors."

—Meyer Lansky on how he would
describe his livelihood.

Philosophizing

"I curse people. Everybody does it. We're human. We're bums. We bums in the street."

—John Gotti.

"… like I say, I know this life, and I know us, and I know love, … but I also have common sense."

—John Gotti.

"Where the fuck are we going here? This is not, ah, yours for keeping. You're gonna die someday. Even, if God forbid, hopefully, it's when you're 95, in your sleep, a heart attack. But, like Angelo, he's gone; you're dead! Gonna go to jail, or some fuckin' thing. Is this what we're working for? To leave a fuckin' mess behind?"

—John Gotti.

"Sometimes, because I was a member of the union, they used to let me wet down all the new brick with a fire hose. I loved doing that. It was fun. I liked to watch the way the brick changed color."

—Henry Hill.

"Everybody has a use. You just have to find out how to use them, find out what they're good for, and put them in the right slot."

—Santo Trafficante.

"That's life. At my age it's too late to worry. What will be, will be."

—Meyer Lansky.

"Some people never learn to be good. One quarter of us is good. Three quarters is bad. That's a tough fight, three against one."

—Meyer Lansky.

"As long as they live through the summertime, what's the difference? Nothing lives forever."

—Dominick "Sonny Black" Napolitano on deciding to buy potted palm trees and ship them to Brooklyn.

"You can't live your whole life on your own. Sooner or later, you're going to get in real trouble or get killed."

—Salvatore "Sammy Bull" Gravano.

"Sometimes, no matter how smart you are, you can't avoid getting tripped up."

—Sammy Bull Gravano.

Philosophizing

"When Scarfo got in, he wanted to use these fuckin' kids. He built a regime and he didn't know what kind of people he had with him. Because he wanted to be a fuckin' movie star. Honor and respect were the things of years ago. Today it's betrayal, deceit, envy, jealousy, viciousness. It's not like it was."

—Nicholas "The Crow" Caramandi.

"When one is born round, he can't die square."

—John Stanfa.

"When you're a dwarf, they could put you on a high mountain, you're still a dwarf."

—Salvatore Avena.

"They can't even shine our shoes, Tommy. That's the situation. And … it's useless. There's a saying that states when a fish starts to smell, it starts from the head. The head has to be cut, otherwise it will smell … I'll kill him … I'll kill him."

—John Stanfa to Tommy Gambino.

"There's always free cheese in the mousetrap."

—Salvatore Avena.

"Here's the only way to do this. We're not gonna be no more patsies 'cause I'm gonna fight everybody around from now on. If a fuckin' general is out in the field with an army, and he's gettin' the shit beat out of him, he has to throw caution to the wind and try stuff, he can't just stand there and get shot down. Any time you become weak you just as well die."

—Murray "Hump" Humphrey
expressing a new philosophy
dealing with the FBI's Top
Hoodlum Program.

"You gotta keep your friends close and your enemies closer."

—Philosophy of Philadelphia mob.

"You can't put the shit back in the donkey."

—John Stanfa paraphrasing
an old Sicilian proverb.

"Everybody asks about that. But I got a God's head on the other side. Everybody has a good side and a bad side."

—John Veasey on the witness stand
when asked about the tattoo of a
devil's head on one side of his chest.

Frank & Fritzy: Fresh Air or Hot Air?

Discussing boss Vincent "Chin" Gigante's penchant for the night moves quickly into a discussion about the relative difference between the air at night and the air in the daytime.

Frank: He's walking in the streets last night. And the dampness. He's crazy, whattaya gonna do?

Fritzy: Well, I'll tell you something. The fuckin' air is cleaner then than during the fuckin' day.

Frank: It's the worst time, they say.

Fritzy: What?

Frank: The night air is no good.

Fritzy: Well, in this city, I gotta disagree with ya'.

Frank: But I know what you mean, but the night air is no good. You're supposed to be in bed before 12 o'clock. Early to bed and early to rise.

Fritzy: Yeah, but, you see, lemme tell you something, that used to be fine and that's true in what you're saying. But as far as breathing air and clean air, that's the hour to breathe it.

Frank: Yeah, it was damp.

Fritzy: I know, but it's still clean air at that hour. Because after 11 o'clock, a lot, you see all the heat, Frankie, all the heat, all the stoves, all the radiators, they shut down. The restaurants, they stop cooking at 10 o'clock. The heat from the buildings, they stop the chimney smoke at 11 o'clock. So it takes about three hours to clear up. So from the hours of, say, 3 o'clock in the morning to about 6 o'clock in the morning, is the cleanest you're ever gonna find it.

Frank: Then you stay up then. It'll be a good idea.

Fritzy: Hey, I gotta, I gotta come out and breathe at night and sleep all day.

Frank: Yeah.

Fritzy: Uh, oogatz. I got one better. Fuck New York, go down to where the air is clean.

Frank: Oh, yeah.

Politics

"Nonsense! He's [Castro] got the mountains. He's a guy making noises up in the hills. He's going nowhere. Don't worry about it. We'll have a good time."

—Santo Trafficante to Frank
Ragano about taking a trip to Cuba.

"Castro is a complete nut! He's not going to be in office or power for long. Either Batista will return or someone else will replace this guy because there's no way the economy can continue without tourists, and this guy is closing all the hotels and casinos. This is a temporary storm. It'll blow over."

—Santo Trafficante.

"Why take a chance on a candidate who might lose. You can always buy them after the election."

—Santo Trafficante's policy of
never contributing to politicians
running for office.

"Did you hear the good news? They killed the son-of-a-bitch bastard. Yeah, he's dead. I heard it over the news that Lyndon Johnson is going to be sworn in as president. You know he'll get rid of Booby [Bobby Kennedy]."

—Jimmy Hoffa.

"Damn right I'm serious. He [Frank Costello] was his partner [Joseph Kennedy, the father of John and Robert Kennedy]. Aren't they hypocritical? Here's this guy, Bobby Kennedy, talking about law and order, and these guys made their goddamn fortune through boot-legging. Bobby Kennedy is stepping on too many toes. Che, you wait and see, somebody is going to kill those sons-of-bitches. It's just a matter of time."

—Santo Trafficante.

"The son-of-a-bitch deserved it, keeping me waiting."

—Jimmy Hoffa explaining his chokehold on Bobby Kennedy.

"You know how the goddamn Kennedys have been hounding me, and you're asking me to honor the President's death?"

—Jimmy Hoffa refusing to fly the flag at half-staff in mourning for JFK.

"I'm a Catholic and I was glad to see a Catholic elected president. I still have some scars left over from growing up and being discriminated against as a Catholic of Italian heritage. On the other hand, I think Bobby Kennedy is an arrogant son-of-a-bitch."

> —Frank Ragano explaining his political views and how he voted in the Kennedy-Nixon race.

"I can't be held accountable for what one underworld figure tells another. It just goes to prove that in an effort to impress each other, they drop names just as any person does."

> —Former Newark mayor Hugh Addonizio, denying that he associated with mobsters who spoke of him as if they knew him.

"We'd like to get a gun permit for this area …. We're trying to stop crime. This is for protection."

> —Simone "Sam the Plumber" DeCavalcante, to a chief of police.

"I cultivated Jimmy Hines right from the beginning. I soon learned that to run an organized mob you've got to have a politician. You have heard about the suspected link between organized crime and politics. Well, I became the missing link."

> —Dutch Schultz about his relationship with Jimmy Hines, a powerful Democratic district leader.

"You're a damn Baptist. Don't you know you've got to know all sorts of people? I use him to do things for me that you wouldn't do."

> —Louis B. Mayer, studio mogul, when a Washington lobbyist refused to join the dinner table and be seen with a gangster.

"Stay low. Don't stir anything up. Keep your head down. You're a sure winner, it ain't like there's going to be a real election here."

> —Advice to Sam Giancana's nephew Anthony DeTolve who was running for alderman.

Frank & Fritzy on Mussolini

Frank: You see *Mussolini* last night?

Fritzy: Oh, yeah. Hey, I always knew you, I told you you were related to him. And I know I'm positive .... Mussolini was a horny bastard ....

Frank: You know, if he would have really ...

Fritzy: Imagine if he don't go with that fuckin' Hitler, what he woulda been, this guy?

Frank: What he woulda been today? Fuhgeddaboutit.

Fritzy: He would have been dead, but he would have been, like, one of the most outstanding men of all time.

Frank: Yeah.

Fritzy: He was that great.

Frank: He would have made Italy one the richest nations ...

Fritzy: He was that great.

Power

"My grandfather, when I was a little boy [told me], 'Salvatore, when strength and reason oppose each other, strength will win and reason becomes worthless.'"

—Salvatore Profaci.

"Gaspar [Lupo] will do anything I tell him. If I tell him to jump off the roof, he'll jump off the fuckin' building."

—Genovese capo James Messera telling his crew that he controlled the president of a New York City Laborers Union Local.

"… if you are not where the strength is, it doesn't matter what you are, all you are is a puppet and they are pulling the fucking strings for you."

—Genovese soldier Vincent Aparo philosophizing about the game of life.

"John [Gotti] had two things going for him. He was loved and feared. He's the only person I've seen with both. You call it charisma. He has that, but love and fear was what counted. People don't cross a man they love and fear."

—Gambino capo Jack D'Amico.

"The men with power are the men with money or the will to take it. They break down into just two classes: the squares and the hustlers. I am a hustler, but I got respect for squares."

—Al Capone.

"I never have to lie to any man because I don't fear anyone. The only time you lie is when you are afraid."

—John Gotti.

"I know everything about Sonny …. I knew what he was and who he was and even who he killed. He was a hitter—the hitter. He swam in the biggest ocean and was the biggest, meanest, most terrifying shark in that ocean."

—Phil Steinberg, young record producer on John "Sonny" Franzese.

"I figured if you were gonna be a mobster, I mean really be a big-time mobster, you had to have steel balls like Sonny Franzese. You had to be able to take out your assassin, then sit there calmly sipping a drink while police wandered about, asking everyone questions. I didn't have balls like that. Hell, nobody had balls like that except Sonny."

—Beau Matera explaining why he moved to Las Vegas rather than join one of the crime families.

"Sonny was what we called an 'ice man.' When he walked into a room, everyone's blood ran cold."

—Phil Steinberg on Sonny.

"We are special people. We are Sicilians. We can kill any people we want."

—Blagio Adornetto.

"Sonny's power had nothing to do with the fact that he was a capo in the Colombo family. Most people didn't know, or didn't care, who he was connected with. His power came from within himself. The neighborhood didn't tremble at the thought of hidden Colombo armies keeping watch—they shook at the sight of Sonny Franzese walking down Thirty-Sixth Avenue."

—Beau Matera whose family owned the Dinner Bell Restaurant in Jackson Heights, Queens.

"If you're gonna kill a snake, you cut off its head. I would have shot (John) Stanfa."

—Blagio Adornetto expressing the opinion that killing the boss made more sense than killing a low-level associate like Joey Ciancaglini.

You Shouldn't Have

Undercover FBI agent Joe Pistone recalls the day he and his fellow undercover operative, Tony Rossi, thought they were giving the Bonanno soldier Lefty Guns Ruggiero a birthday present.

"You always exchange birthday and Christmas presents with guys you're close to in the crew. It's expected. This day I don't say anything. I don't even wish Lefty happy birthday. I just let him stew.

"All day he's asking me, 'Donnie, didn't you forget something today? Isn't something supposed to happen today?'

"'Nothing I can think of. Everything's under control.'

"Finally, at ten o'clock that night, he and Rossi and I are sitting at our round table at the club and Lefty is grumpy. I say, 'Lefty! I forgot! It's your birthday!'

"'Hey, that's right.' He grins.

"I lean over and give him a kiss and hand him an envelope. In it, wrapped in tissue, are seven diamonds, confiscated by the FBI. 'This is from Tony [Rossi] and me. Happy birthday!'

"He opens it. 'Aw, Donnie, you didn't have to do this. What a great present! I'll give one to my wife, one to each daughter, one to each grandchild.'

"'Tony and me figured you're worth it.'

"'Aw, gee.' He gives me a big hug and kiss. 'What's Tony giving me?'

"Rossi is sitting right there.

"'The diamonds are from both of us,' I say.

"'Donnie, I can't tell you, that's the nicest present. That's why I love you. You make mistakes, but times like this are just—What about Tony, he forget?'

"'Lefty, we are both giving you this.'

"'Is Tony gonna give me anything?'

"Finally, Rossi gets up, goes into the office, puts three $100 bills in an envelope, comes back, and gives it to Lefty. 'Happy birthday, Lefty,' he says.

"'Aw, Tony, you didn't have to do this. You could have shared with Donnie and both give me the diamonds, that would have been enough.'"

Prison Life

"I've been in the system for years and I've always been allowed to wear this."

—DeCavalcante soldier James Gallo complaining about being ordered to take off his silver jewelry as he removed it from his neck and handed it to a woman before being led off to federal prison for murder.

"Even a mediocre fighter would be left alone if he put up violent resistance. The wolves had too much easy prey to bother with a guy who resisted."

—Eddie Maloney describing the tactics he used to survive in prison.

"Joe said he'd built a false partition underneath a delivery truck, wedged himself in, and rode out to safety. The cops said they'd forget to file charges if he told them how he did it, but Joe wouldn't talk."

—Eddie Maloney describing "Mad Dog" Joe Sullivan's escape from Attica prison.

"The prisoner portion of the Zephyr Cove Jail con-
sisted of a single medium-sized cell, which the cop said
was built for six. I counted five guys when he pushed
me inside, but I didn't think a NO VACANCY sign would
light up now that it was full."

—Eddie Maloney.

"Leave the country, do anything, Frank, just don't go
to prison. They take away your self-respect, your dignity. You've got guys who couldn't shine your shoes on
the outside, telling you when you can eat and sleep and
even take a shit."

—Jimmy Hoffa on life behind bars.

"Right from the beginning you could see that life in
the can was different for wiseguys. Everybody else was
doing real time, all mixed together, living like pigs.
Wiseguys lived alone."

—Henry Hill.

"Saturday—Just for going out with a fellow, look where
I am. Monday—Finally learned how to make my blan-
kets like a sack so they don't fall off at night. Hope I
remember stories I heard in here … Thursday—New
witnesses are very nice. Learned how to play coon-can
and whist."

—Excerpt from a diary that Pittsburgh
Phil's girlfriend Evelyn Mittelman kept
during her six-week-long stay in the
Women's House of Detention.

"To get past the prison guards, I sewed food in sacks and strapped them to my body. The guards would search our bags and make us walk through the metal detectors, looking for knives and guns, but that's all they did. As long as you didn't wrap anything in aluminum foil, you could walk in with a grocery store under your coat. I used to wear a big poncho, and I had sandwiches and salami and stuff from my feet to my chin. I used to put pint bottles of brandy and Scotch in a pair of extra-large and extra-wide boots I bought just for getting past the gate. I got a giant-size forty-two-DD bra and a pair of leg girdles to carry the pot and pills. I used to walk into the visiting room as stiff as the Tin Man, but the guards didn't mind."

—Karen Hill, on visiting Henry in prison.

"You learn a lot of shit in prison. It seems like everybody's got a personality clash. The guys from New York, Harlem, don't like the guys from Brooklyn. The guys from Brooklyn don't like the guys from Manhattan. The guys from Manhattan don't like the guys from Harlem. It's one vicious circle with these New York guys. But basically most of them were pretty decent to me."

—Nicholas "The Crow" Caramandi.

"And you hear everybody's story. Everybody's innocent. Everybody got ratted out. Every day you heard a different fuckin' story. Guys stole their whole lives and they get caught for one beef and they're crying."

—The Crow Caramandi.

"The MDC officials were losing control of the prison and the people who were running the prison [block] were the inmates."

—Assistant U.S. attorney Pam Davis describing how Colombo capo Wild Bill Cutolo and his crew had taken over the Metropolitan Detention Center as they awaited trial for racketeering and murder.

"He's like the bag of golf clubs sitting in my closet."

—Correction officer describing Steve "The Rifleman" Flemmi in his prison cell.

"Hey, I don't recall sending you a resumé for a job. I'm just a prisoner. I'm not taking over anything. In fact, you can keep me in lockdown twenty-four hours if you want. I just want to do my time in peace.

—Michael "The Yuppie Don" Franzese to the prison's chief lieutenant.

"When little Odierno was in the Death House I sent him dough so he could have cigarettes and stuff. Hell, you can't be mad at a guy when he's in that place."

—Dutch Schultz.

"I can't believe all they say of him. In my seven years' experience, I have never seen a prisoner so kin, cheery, and accommodating. He does his work—that of a file clerk—faithfully and with a high degree of intelligence. He has brains. He would have made good anywhere, at anything. He has been an ideal prisoner."

—Dr. Herbert M. Goddard of the
Pennsylvania State Board of Prison
Inspectors, describing Al Capone.

"And don't worry about us going to jail. Me number one! I like jail better than I like the streets. And do what I'm tellin' ya. And don't ever have these kind of meetings again."

—John Gotti reminding lawyer
Gerald Shargel that Gotti and his
men don't plead guilty to anything.

"If you buy a pound of beef and grind it yourself, that's better yet, as you will know it is fresh. As you roll the meat on the palms of your hands, you keep putting a little olive oil on your palms, to prevent the meat from sticking. Make the meatballs any size you want."

> —Joseph Valachi, who was such a
> good cook that prison guards would
> ask him to write his recipes for
> their wives, with some helpful hints
> on the art of making meatballs.

"Right now, give me a prosciutto sandwich with ricotta insalade cheese. Give me some prosciutto with mozzarella or Swiss cheese. Provolone, give me that, with a couple hot peppers on a Sicilian loaf of seeded bread, right now, I will let you hit me with fucking scaling pipes right down the middle of my fucking head. For one of them fucking sandwiches right now, I'll be like a fucking baby."

> —John Gotti telling brother Pete
> what he would do if he could get
> some real Italian food at Marion
> Federal Penitentiary.

Food for Thought

A jailhouse conversation in which mob associate Sam Cagnina enlightens Jose Reyes about Frankie No and Rao's, a popular Italian restaurant in East Harlem that is a favorite of politicians, celebrities, and gangsters.

Cagnina: I know that guy took his table the other day, at Rao's. That restaurant that nobody, nobody could get into .... Two or three tables, only actors got that. You can't go there. I don't give a fuck who you are or how much money you have.

Reyes: I remember, [UI] there's only like, let's say ten tables.

Cagnina: Yeah. And nobody can get in .... Don't give a fuck who you are. I don't care who you are. But like I say, Donald Trump has got one. Actors got one .... And Gambinos got two tables or three. Vincent had the most, he had three tables ....

Reyes: So that's the only way they get their business, no?

Cagnina: A lot of people go there. And they sell, no, they sell sauce, too. To the people outside. It's the best sauce made.

Reyes: That restaurant is that famous?

Cagnina: It's on the radio and TV all the time. Rao's. They call Frankie, "No." Frankie No No. You know, Frankie No, they call him. That's this guy runs it. You know why they call him that? Because he says "no" to everybody. Don't have an opening. Even if you call for reservations, he says no. I hear it on TV all the time and on the radio. I've seen a guy on the radio in there on Imus .... It's called Rao's. *Understand?*

Respect

"The most important thing: respect. The worst thing you can do is embarrass a wiseguy. If you embarrass a captain or a boss, forget about it. You're history."

—Lefty Guns Ruggiero to Joe
"Donnie Brasco" Pistone.

"… a don right out of Central Casting. He was a tough, gritty man who stood 5-foot-seven and ate, drank and slept the mob."

—Michael "The Yuppie Don" Franzese
on Carmine "Junior" Persico.

"He's got balls. He walked in and killed the two garbage guys in broad daylight."

—Anthony "Bowat" Baratta praising
the work of Luchese soldier Frank
"Frankie Pearl" Federico in killing
two unarmed businessmen at 6 A.M.

Respect

"Honor is the most important thing in the world. Respect and honor. You've got to keep your word because if you don't have honor and respect, you don't have anything."

—Santo Trafficante after Frank
Ragano promised Santo that he could
sponsor his second child as a godfather.

"John was the boss; I was the underboss. John barked and I bit."

—Salvatore "Sammy Bull"
Gravano at the murder and
racketeering trial of John Gotti.

"I tell ya something, Michael. You got some balls. If I were in your shoes, I don't know if I could have taken it. You were ice. Man, you were ice. You sat in this car like you were going to dinner."

—Vincent "Jimmy" Angellino to
The Yuppie Don Franzese who
was called to a sit-down.

"Let the bum go. He cheated me fair and square"

—Joseph "Joe Batters" Accardo, after a
pool shark had hustled him for $1,000.

"When a dispute arose in regards to the distribution of skim between Milwaukee and Kansas City, Chicago settled the dispute and began receiving 25 percent of the skim."

—Angelo Lonardo telling a Senate Committee that Milwaukee and Kansas City answered to Chicago.

"When Tony and I went there the boss always gave us a table by ourselves. He never sat anyone nearby because we didn't want anyone on the eary. Around our table there was nothing but white tablecloths, even if the joint was crowded."

—Frank Cullotta describing how he and Anthony "The Ant" Spilotro always got a table by themselves so no one could eavesdrop on their conversation.

"By then John had come up, and he looks at John and says, 'Oh, Mr. Rosselli, of course, we have your table.' It was just stunning. I saw this crew come running out and set up this extra table, in an alcove, they had to move another over, just to make room. I've never seen anything like it in my life. Johnny never said a thing. And I know we didn't have a reservation."

—Attorney Leslie Scherr describing a visit to a packed, fancy Italian restaurant with Johnny Rosselli.

Respect

"He's the finest man I ever met."

—James Cardinali, a prosecution
witness describing John Gotti.

"From a distance I thought Dellacroce, seated alone at a table, resembled someone's harmless white-haired grandfather. The illusion faded when we were face to face. The flat, dead eyes—a killer's eyes—gave him away."

—Eddie Maloney describing his
meeting with Aniello Dellacroce.

 Frank & Fritzy on Finances and Face

Fritzy: If I had, I owed my fuckin' money, I'd take all the rings, everything I got and I'd go and sell 'em and say, "Here, lemme pay my debts."

Frank: Yeah.

Fritzy: Who the fuck? What kinda? I'll tell ya one thing. The day I live and the day I die, when I die, nobody's gonna come and say, "The man owed me ten thousand. The man owed me two thousand." I will go to work before it ever comes ....

Frank: You got a heart of gold, Fritzy.

Fritzy: No, pa, look. The heart is one thing.

Frank: You gotta heart of fuckin' gold.

Fritzy: Ya hear what I says?

Frank: [UI] make a fool out of you.

Fritzy: Cal, the heart is one thing. The second thing is [In Italian, the face].

Frank: Yeah, I know ...

Fritzy: [In Italian, the face. The face] is more important.

Frank: Yeah.

Fritzy: In other words, [UI] they got [In Italian, the face of a whore]. They don't give a fuck one way or the other, "Well, yeah. Okay." I gotta have somebody belittle me.

Frank: Yeah.

Fritzy: And while I know I'm [UI], ya gotta know how to co, how to handle them people, you know what I mean? You know, that, that's their game. That's the way. "Alright, fine." There's just so much you, you do. And just so much that comes and reverse.

Retirement

"This business we're in, you get old fast, and a lot of things you do now you can't do when you get older. Donnie, take some of that money and give it to that friend and have them keep it for you. So when you get older and can't be out stealing every day, you got yourself a nice little stash. You don't have to worry about being old and broke."

—Bonanno associate Fort Lee
Jimmy Capasso recommending a
Mafia-style retirement plan in 1977.

"I know what I did all of my life. Love it! And if they gave me a second shot, I'd do it all over again."

—Lawyer Mike Coiro.

"Naturally, if I could do my life over again, I would. Who would not? Now I am all alone in this world. As you know, I do not write to my wife and my son as they will have nothing to do with me and I don't blame them."

—Joseph Valachi.

"I'm not running from the fucking Mafia. I was a boxer. I know what it's like to get hit. I know what it is to fight. You lose your fear. I could go to Montana and live 20 years in a cabin and be scared to death. Or I can live here [in Arizona] … I choose to live here."

—Salvatore "Sammy Bull" Gravano.

"The hardest thing for me [about going into the witness protection program] was leaving the life I was running away from. Even at the end, with all the threats I was getting and all the time I was facing behind the wall, I still loved the life."

—Henry Hill.

"Once you're in the racket, you're in it for life. Your past holds you in it. The gang won't let you out. And me settle down? Don't make me laugh. If I did, I'd get mine so quick at the end of a sawed-off shotgun it would be nobody's business …. Murder, murder—that's all this racket means. I'm sick of it. I'd give half my fortune to get out of it. If I could go to Florida and live quietly with my family for the rest of my days, I'd be the happiest man alive."

—Al Capone.

"You don't get released from my crew. You have lived with John Gotti and you will die with John Gotti."

—John Gotti.

Retirement

"There is a lure to being an informer that generates an excitement, a thrill, I'm going to miss."

—Turncoat mob associate
Joseph Cantalupo.

"Once you are admitted into this mob and you take this oath there is no way you can quit. The only way you can go out, you get killed. There is no retirement."

—Nicholas "The Crow" Caramandi.

"Right now, I'm cursed. I'm stuck in this joint and that's the end of it. This is my realm, right here. That's the end of it."

—John Gotti.

"I'm gonna get a spot as a warden at some little jail upstate. I know how to treat prisoners .... I could reform them."

—Abe "Kid Twist" Reles.

"I am going to build and buy a home here [in Miami] and I hope that many of my friends will join me. Furthermore, if I am permitted, I will open the finest restaurant anywhere in the state and if I am invited I will even join your Rotary Club."

—Al Capone.

"I'd do it legal. I learned too late that you need just as good a brain to make a crooked million as an honest million. These days, you apply for a license to steal from the public. If I had my time again, I'd make sure I got that license first."

—Meyer Lansky.

"The devil didn't make me do it. I did it on my own."

—Sammy Bull Gravano.

Stealing

"... and then Tony got a white towel and put it on the kitchen table. Then Nancy bent over the table, and one by one she began dropping diamonds out of her hair. They kept coming out one after another. He had made her hide them there. The customs people might have confiscated some of the diamonds, but I think the prize stones got through in Nancy's beehive."

—Frank Cullotta after picking Anthony "The Ant" Spilotro up at the airport.

"It turns out there were a couple of heist guys specializing in maitre d's because their pockets are filled with twenty dollar bills."

—Frank Cullotta.

"Burke loved to steal. Nothing made him happier, and he enjoyed the company of other thieves. He even named his two sons Frank James Burke and Jesse James Burke."

—Eddie Maloney describing Jimmy "The Gent" Burke, mastermind of the Lufthansa heist.

"It was exactly the kind of score I hoped for to fund my Florida retirement plans in grand style."

—Eddie Maloney.

"Please don't tell my father. Please. I'll never do it again."

—Eight-year-old Salvatore Gravano to a Bensonhurst, Brooklyn store owner who caught him stealing two cupcakes on his way to school.

"The thing you've got to understand about Jimmy is that he loved to steal. He ate and breathed it. I think if you ever offered Jimmy a billion dollars not to steal, he'd turn you down and then try to figure out how to steal it from you. It was the only thing he enjoyed. It kept him alive."

—Henry Hill.

"The Varios had more than enough money to buy the store a hundred times over. It was just that stuff that was stolen always tasted better than anything bought. The real thrill of the night for Paulie, his biggest pleasure, was that he was robbing someone and getting away with it."

—Henry Hill.

Stealing

"Most of the loads hijacked were sold before they were even robbed. They were hijacks to order."

—Henry Hill.

"The story I loved best about Old Man Paruta was one Frank DeCicco would tell. It seems that in his early days, Frank was going on a robbery with some guys. And for this particular score, they needed a lock picker. Somebody told Frank that Paruta was just the person they were looking for. Frank was surprised. He said to Paruta, 'How come I haven't heard this before about you?' Old Man Paruta just smiled and said there wasn't a better lock guy around than him. So they're in the place and Frank nods at Paruta, who steps forward and what he does is, he kicks in the door. 'See, what did I tell you?' Paruta says. Frank was stunned. He couldn't stop laughing."

—Salvatore "Sammy Bull" Gravano.

"I don't mind that you're a thief. I'm a thief. I don't mind you stealing, but you can't rob from us."

—Gene Gotti dressing down a crook who was caught in the act stealing a school bus laden with adding machines and typewriters from an Ozone Park company the Gotti crew controlled.

Three Strikes

Defense Attorney: When you were growing up, did you learn the Ten Commandments?

Nicholas "The Crow" Caramandi: Yes.

Attorney: Did you learn "Thou shalt not steal"?

Caramandi: Yes.

Attorney: "Thou shalt not kill"?

Caramandi: Yes.

Attorney: "Thou shalt not lie"?

Caramandi: Yes.

Attorney: The three commandments I just mentioned, how many of them did you break?

Caramandi: I broke them all.

Style

"Not unlike corporate officers, guys on the upper rungs of the crime ladder put stock in how a young gangster looked. If an up-and-comer dressed well, he had 'class.' He might be dismissed as a 'bum' if he didn't wear presentable threads."

—Eddie Maloney.

"Get a haircut and take a bath, and I might give you a ride next time."

—Meyer Lansky's advice to a hitchhiker from his car.

"You like it? Here. It's yours. If you don't take it, you'll offend me."

—Santo Trafficante to Frank Ragano after Frank complimented his tie.

"Stop buying suits and jackets off the racks in ordinary stores because ten other men will wear the identical clothes."

> —Santo Trafficante advising Frank
> Ragano to obtain his clothes
> from a tailor in Miami Beach.

"The only people who wear blue suits with brown shoes are queers and FBI men."

> —Santo Trafficante.

"Take that tie off, cut it up and throw it away. I don't care how much it cost. And don't go near that shop again."

> —Salvatore "Sammy Bull" Gravano
> to Lou Vallario, after a furious
> John Gotti complained that
> Big Lou had just bought the
> same $200 tie as Gotti.

"The next time I see you, I want to see you with some teeth."

> —Vito Genovese to a lowly
> toothless enforcer whose
> appearance displeased him.

Frank & Fritzy: Shop 'Til You Drop

Fritzy: I took my daughter shopping this morning. I went to the Banana Republic. I bought clothes for the safari.

Frank: No kiddin'.

Fritzy: Yeah.

Frank: The Banana Republic.

Fritzy: Yeah, sure.

Frank: You bought a lot of things there?

Fritzy: I bought, uh, a few pairs of khakis, you know.

Frank: No kidding.

Fritzy: Yeah.

Frank: And what else?

Fritzy: Uh, the kids, the kids, I bought her a bomber jacket …

Frank: Yeah.

Fritzy: I bought a, a, a Charles Lindbergh, uh, hat. When ya', when he flew the Atlantic.

Frank: Yeah.

Fritzy: I bought a hat with the goggles, I bought for myself.

Frank: No kiddin'.

Fritzy: Yeah.

Frank: And a hat with the goggles?

Fritzy: Yeah, this way, if I fly, ya' know, when I go flying with my airplane I'll wear it.

Talking Trash

"My name isn't Spilotray, you motherfucker. You never saw me in your life. And Frank Rosenthal wasn't here either. And if I hear you telling anything to anybody, this place is going to become a bowling alley and you're gonna be in the fucking racks."

—Anthony "The Ant" Spilotro
to a restaurant owner who
introduced himself.

"Still he keeps it up. 'Fuck you, asshole,' he says. I'm standing there in the woods with a gun on him. I'm over six feet and weigh two hundred and twenty pounds. If he's been tailing me he knows I work out boxing every day at the Y. Meanwhile, he's five five and a hundred and thirty-five pounds, and he's busting my balls in a secluded spot in the park. That was Tony. He dared you to murder him."

—FBI agent William Roemer
about The Ant Spilotro.

"After that, whenever I talked to my friends in the press about Spilotro, I always referred to him as 'that little pissant.' [Reporters] began using the name 'the Ant' when they wrote about him. I guess in those days, 'pissant' was not proper for the public press."

—FBI agent William Roemer about
The Ant Spilotro.

"They're not going to do anything to me. If they want to kill me they're going to kill me, but they're not going to scare me. Let's just sit down and have some breakfast."

—Tom Wadden describing Johnny
Rosselli's fearless attitude.

"I got a chalk and drew a line down the center of the union hall, and said, 'All right, this is how we're going about this election. All those in favor of my being president step on this side of the line; all those in favor of the weasel step on the other side of the line. Because tonight we're going to separate the rat shit from the raisins.'"

—Jimmy Hoffa, at the age of nineteen, making a motion to elect a new president of a Detroit local.

"You deny everything! The only thing we tell the truth about is our name. And we tell it to the lawyer."

> —John Gotti telling his men what to say if they are arrested.

"I would have shaved. I want to show some respect."

> —Joseph Valachi on why he was so upset when biographer Peter Maas arrived unannounced to interview him for the book he was writing about Valachi's life.

"Let me tell you something, Fitz. You know I don't like someone pissing on my leg and telling me it's raining."

> —Jimmy Hoffa complaining to Frank Fitzsimmons.

"What are you gonna do? They blame everything on us, anyway. They'll blame that one on us."

> —John Gotti.

"We're nice guys. We don't have to duck nobody. You're the ones who should be duckin', the way you treat people."

> —John Gotti, to FBI agents.

"Jimmy could corrupt a saint. He said bribing cops was like feeding elephants at a zoo. 'All you need is peanuts.'"

—Henry Hill on his old friend,
Jimmy "The Gent" Burke.

"Wiseguys like Paulie have been paying off the cops for so many years that they have probably sent more cops' kids to college than anyone else. They're like wiseguy scholarships."

—Henry Hill on Paul Vario.

"I saw this guy in a windbreaker who popped up along-side the car and jammed a gun against the side of my head. For a second I thought it was over. Then he screamed, 'Make one move, motherfucker, and I'll blow you away!' That's when I began to relax. That's when I knew they were cops. Only cops talk that way. If it had been wiseguys, I wouldn't have heard a thing. I would have been dead."

—Henry Hill on his arrest.

"He used to make me nuts. Day after day going over the same stuff. Every detail. Every question. He was a real pain in the ass."

—Nicholas "The Crow" Caramandi,
describing Louis Pichini, the lead
prosecutor for whom Caramandi
testified in a racketeering case.

"All guilty, all charges. I guess that means I'm credible."

> —Caramandi, on the night the jury
> convicted Nicodemo "Little Nicky"
> Scarfo and 16 codefendants on
> every charge in the indictment.

"Our law is a law that you know is gonna get results. They know when they come with a problem and they sit down and they explain their problem, no matter how difficult, we're right there to help them."

> —Caramandi, on why some people
> go to the mob instead of the police
> when they need help.

"Thank God for the American jury system."

> —Philadelphia boss Nicky
> Scarfo to reporters.

"It's difficult being a gentleman around here."

> —John Gotti, on a day things
> didn't go well in court.

"You know how they say I'm Bruce's [Cutler] only client the last eight years. Well, I'm Gleeson's only case. This guy, you know what he says when he wakes up in the morning, rolls over and looks at his wife? He says, 'Hiya, John.' This guy learned to talk listening to my voice! I'd like to have a bug on him for three hours."

—John Gotti, with two different versions of the same idea about federal prosecutor John Gleeson.

"We don't know nothing ourselves. We hear it the same place you get it. We get it from the FBI."

—John Gotti, responding to questions about whether he was the boss of the Gambino crime family.

"What the fuck they want you to do? Hang out with doctors and lawyers?"

—Bonanno wiseguy Joseph Massino after Gambino soldier Angelo Ruggiero told him that FBI agents were stopping guys who visited him.

"They have no case. If my kids ever lied as much as these guys lied, they'd have no dinner."

—John Gotti, complaining about police officers testifying against him.

"Mendacity. The word for today is mendacity. It's the art of being mendacious."

—John Gotti making the same complaint on another day.

"The police in the station were so thick that some of them were pretending to sell apples."

—Al Capone using an interesting analogy to make the point that there were lots of cops at the train station in Los Angeles.

"The police have told me a lot of stories. They shoved a lot of murders over me. They did it because they couldn't find the men who did the jobs, and I looked like an easy goat."

—Al Capone to reporters.

"I've been spending the best years of my life as a public benefactor. I've given people the light pleasures, shown them a good time. And all I get is abuse—the existence of a hunted man. I'm called a killer. Well, tell the folks I'm going away now. I guess murder will stop. There won't be any more booze. You won't be able to find a crap game, even, let alone a roulette wheel or a faro game."

—Al Capone to reporters.

"That cocksucker! That's open territory. Who is he [Joe Bonanno] to put a fuckin' flag up there and claim squatter's rights."

—Chicago mob boss Tony Accardo
complaining about Joe Bonanno's
claim to Tucson, Arizona.

"Who gave Louisiana to Frank Costello?"

—Crazy Joe Gallo, questioning
the status quo.

"You got balls, come on. Come on, you need to kill me, kill me you little punk."

—Colombo capo Joseph Scopo as he
threw a cell phone at John Pappa and
dared him to kill him, seconds before
Pappa shot him to death.

"This guy is a mutt, period, plain and simple."

—Brooklyn federal judge Raymond
Dearie, describing prosecution witness
Ronald "Messy Marvin" Moran.

"Alright. There's something called the 'Know Your Client Rule.' Now I don't expect you to know everything about your client, but I do expect you to know when your client is fucking alive or dead. Now this guy Rogers died on Dec. 1. There were 11 trades done after Dec. 1. His executor is calling up the company asking for an explanation ...."

—Mob-connected stock fraud artist Frank Persico complaining to his stable of corrupt brokers about their lack of attention to detail.

 Frank & Fritzy: The Pear in the Hat?

Fritzy: Did he give you the hat? Did he give you that hat?

Frank: What hat?

Fritzy: That hat you had on.

Frank: Which hat?

Fritzy: You had a hat on. The gray hat.

Frank: Who give me?

Fritzy: I'm askin'. Did he give you the hat?

Frank: He gave me shit.

Fritzy: He had one. Somebody brought 'em two, three hats, had one just like it.

Frank: No, but he gives ice away in the winter. He loads up with fuckin' clothes that he's got he never wears.

Fritzy: Yeah, well he's wearin' that coat, uh.

Frank: Yeah, he's wearin', he'll wear that out. He'll keep wearin' and wearin' and wearin' and wearin' and wearin' it. You ever see 'em with pants? He wears one pair of pants.

Fritzy: Yeah. So then when he wears it out ...

Frank: Bring 'em to the cleaners, he bring 'em back, he says, "What the fuck did they do to my pants. They ruined 'em." He's in them fuckin' pants sittin' that big ass in that chair.

Fritzy: He got, he's got a little [In Italian, ass] now.

Frank: Night and day in that ass. Well, he's built like a pear, whattaya [UI]. Marone, he's broad down there.

Fritzy: Yeah.

Frank: He's still broad.

Fritzy: So how you doin'?

Frank: Alright, Freddie.

Threats

"Happy Birthday, share the cake."

> —An angry birthday greeting New
> Jersey boss John Riggi sent to
> family consigliere Steven Vitabile
> to let him know he was furious that
> Vitabile wasn't sending enough
> of his profits to the boss.

"I'll give it to you in three ways—get out, stay out, or
be rubbed out."

> —Dutch Schultz telling Otto Gass
> to withdraw from the beer business.

"It's always much better not to shoot if you can help it.
It's better to use reason—or if that fails, threats."

> —Meyer Lansky.

Threats

"You was happy callin' in them fuckin' bets. I mean, it's unbelievable. You was nice and happy when you were callin' the fuck in. Now, all of a sudden, what, what am I gonna do? … You know what I mean. You wanna bet. You wanna act like a fuckin' man, you gotta be like a man now. You gotta come up with the fuckin' money somehow."

—Mob enforcer Tommy Marrone to a
college student who owed $3,925.

"Can you imagine that cocksucker? He don't know if he wants to do me a favor? Keep your eye on him, Butch. If he comes through, fine. If not, we cut the balls off his business."

—Sam "Momo" Giancana after asking
wealthy Chicago industrialist Angelo
Girabaldi to wine and dine FBI agents
to gather information for Sam.

"I won the sit-down. You don't pay nobody but me."

—Bonanno capo Thomas DiFiore
telling the owner of an adult entertainment porn shop that he would be
paying protection money to DiFiore,
not the Gambino family, or else.

"I'd like you guys to spread the word. Tell the rest of your people just exactly what happened. Rocky De Grazia beat up one of ours, we retaliated. Remember that phrase if you will—'retribution in kind'. You throw a shot, we'll throw one, too. We've got eight thousand FBI agents in this country, about three hundred of 'em right here in Chicago. Anytime you think about starting something, think about that. Take this back to all your people. We want this clearly understood."

—FBI agent William Roemer Jr.

"You don't have no alternative. We want something now. And you're lucky it ain't more. This is a serious request. You understand? What are we playin', a fuckin' game here, pal? You reaped the harvest all those fuckin' years! This is something you're going to pay now. We want it. We're not asking."

—Mob enforcer Dennis
Lepore shaking down 89-year-old
"Doc" Sagansky, millionaire
Boston bookmaker.

"Whatever happened in the past is over. There is to be no more ill feeling among us. If you lost someone in this past war of ours, you must forgive and forget. If your own brother was killed, don't try to find out who did it to get even. If you do, you pay with your life."

—Powerful Mafia leader Salvatore
Maranzano shortly before he was
killed by gangsters who disagreed
with him quite strongly.

"I gotta get that ballpeen hammer ... the Italian hammer. Then, when they talk, you give them the circle right in the forehead."

—Philadelphia boss Ralph Natale
on the art of keeping people quiet.

Violence

"Murder was the only way everybody stayed in line. It was the ultimate weapon. Nobody was immune. You got out of line, you got whacked."

> —Henry Hill on life with Jimmy
> "The Gent" Burke and Paul Vario.

"I love the smell of gunpowder."

> —Colombo capo Greg Scarpa Sr.
> after a shooting.

"The bomb was fuckin' something. The car was bombed like they put gasoline on it. You gotta see the car. You wouldn't believe the car."

> —John Gotti describing the after-
> math of the bomb blast that killed
> underboss Frank DeCicco.

"Sometimes I was the shooter. Sometimes I was a backup shooter. Sometimes I set the guy up. Sometimes I just talked about it. When you go out on a piece of work, it doesn't matter what position you're in."

> —Salvatore "Sammy Bull" Gravano.

Violence

"You could see the dust coming off his jacket when the bullets hit."

> —Bastiano "Buster" Domingo
> describing the killing of Joseph
> "Joe Baker" Catania in 1931.

"Look at this. Now we can kill guys without bullets. They use their own guns. That's how afraid they are of us."

> —Philadelphia wiseguy Salvie Testa
> bragging how Enrico Riccobene
> killed himself out of fear.

"I couldn't move him. Boobie [Cerasani] could. Trin was all cut open and bleeding. There was little pieces lying around from the shotgun [blast]. Boobie got blood all over him trying to pick him up. I couldn't believe how strong Boobie is. He don't look it. But I was amazed. Boobie could move him. Then they cut him up and put him in green plastic garbage bags."

> —Benjamin "Lefty Guns"
> Ruggiero describing what
> happened to Dominick
> "Big Trin" Trinchera in 1981.

"If you don't do the right thing, the man with the green eyes will come to see you."

> —A macabre expression describing Santo Trafficante's green eyes and reputation in Tampa's Italian neighborhood.

"Anybody can use a gun. The Hump uses his head. He can shoot if he has to, but he likes to negotiate with cash when he can. I like that in a man."

> —Al Capone, about his protégé Murray "Hump" Humphrey.

"You were brought up with fear …. They would kill you if you opened your mouth."

> —Grazia Antonucci, describing Al Capone and his men.

"It was either kill or be killed."

> —Nicholas "The Crow" Caramandi.

"In a hit, pulling the trigger is the easy part. Because it takes no brains."

> —Sammy Bull Gravano.

"A little violence never hurt anybody."

> —Lefty Guns Ruggiero.

"There's so many fucking stool pigeons that you can't kill them all. You need Castro's army to kill all the stool pigeons in Milwaukee."

—Steve DiSalvo.

"When John Gotti wanted you dead, he wanted you dead yesterday. That way, he could walk around and look like he's so fucking ferocious."

—Sammy Bull Gravano.

"When we were in a fight Benny would never hesitate. He was even quicker to take action than those hot-blooded Sicilians, the first to start punching and shooting. Nobody reacted faster than Benny."

—Meyer Lansky talking about his old friend, Benjamin "Bugsy" Siegel, whose friends called him Ben or Benny and whom acquaintances called Mr. Siegel, if they knew what was good for them.

"Ain't a fucking man in New York City would go up against me one on one, because I would do it cowboy-style, right on South Street, one block walking at each other. How many pistols you want? Two? Let's walk up against each other. One of us got to fucking die, or both of us die. That's what I would do. I wouldn't give a fuck, and don't forget it."

—Lefty Guns Ruggiero.

"I wouldn't have minded going to Vietnam. You got medals for killing people there."

—Sammy Bull Gravano.

"Violence is bad business. Violence will destroy us. Peace is profitable."

—Michael "The Yuppie Don" Franzese.

"I'd tie him to a chair, okay? Then I'd take a baseball bat, and I'd take my best swing across his fuckin' head. I'd watch his head come off his shoulders. Then I'd take a chainsaw and cut his fuckin' toes off."

—John "Red" Shea describing what he would do if he found an informant.

"I shoot the guy. I don't remember how many times. The poor guy, he was crying. He say, 'Rosario, why you do this to me?' I said, 'Don't make this harder for me.' I shoot him. Then I got out of the car, took him out, and just left him there."

—Rosario Bellocchi, Sicilian-born hitman, on his first mob killing.

Violence

"Meester Johnny Stanfa said to me, 'You must use the lupara.' He said it would send a message because the Sicilian Mafia uses the lupara. He said go right in his face. Blow his head off. That way there would be no mistake."

—Rosario Bellocchi explaining
why he used a sawed-off
shotgun known as a lupara.

"He [John Stanfa] said he wanted to kill him, cut his penis off, put it in his mouth, and leave his body on Delaware Avenue ... to show people he had talked too much."

—Rosario Bellocchi.

"So Big Ralph was very bitter about being stabbed, and he always said that someday he would get even. But I said to him, 'You better forget about even. There is no fuckin' even.'"

—The Crow Caramandi.

"These guys don't ever forget."

—John LaMonte, FBI witness
against Vastola and Levy, explaining
why he continues to live in fear.

"So the idiot follows, still cursing and threatening Sonny. Now I'm getting mad. I'm about to deck the guy when Sonny holds me back. He shakes his head, shrugs, and talks in a soft, calm voice: 'Phil, let it go— let it go. Who cares? He's nothing. We don't have to do anything. Guys like that, somebody will do it for you.'"

—Phil Steinberg describing
how John "Sonny" Franzese
handled an encounter with
a guy at a boxing match.

 Frank and Fritzy on Respect for the Dead

Frank: You sending him a flower?

Fritzy: Yeah.

Frank: Why don't you send one for me, too, huh?

Fritzy: Yeah?

Frank: That would be nice.

Fritzy: That would be nice?

Frank: Yeah, you … 'cause I got no flower guy. I called the guy …

Fritzy: You got a flower guy. What happened to your flower guy?

Frank: He don't deliver to the Bronx.

Fritzy: My flower guy sends, uh, flowers with birds.

Frank: I know it.

Fritzy: And you keep robbing my birds. Alright, I'll take care of it tomorrow.

Frank: "Helen and Frankie."

Fritzy: "Helen and Frankie." Okay. How much you wanna spend?

Frank: About six hundred.

Fritzy: Don't give me that fuck, how much you wanna spend?

Frank: [UI]

Fritzy: [In Italian, says $100.]

Frank: Two hundred, like that, you know?

Fritzy: You want … yeah?

Frank: A hundred and fifty.

Fritzy: A hundred fifty, alright, a hundred fifty's enough.

Frank: Don't make it look better than yours, I know that.

Fritzy: I'll keep it the same. Alright … two $150 flowers.

Frank: That what you sent, that what they cost you?

Fritzy: No. The one I sent you cost me three hundred.

Frank: No kiddin'?

Fritzy: Sure, the one with the birds.

Frank: That's beautiful, huh?

Fritzy: Sure, what's the matter with you?

Frank: Right.

Fritzy: He ain't getting, this guy ain't getting no $300 flower.

Frank: No.

Fritzy: [UI] I think we go for a hundred apiece.

Wiseass Comments

"The canary could sing, but he couldn't fly."

> —Anthony "Nino" Gaggi crying out
> in glee about the death of informer
> Abe "Kid Twist" Reles, who fell to
> his death from a hotel window.

"They got two chairs, Jerry. We can hold hands together. I won't go any other way."

> —Boston Capo Larry Zannino in a bit
> of gallows humor saying he didn't
> want to be electrocuted without
> Gennaro Angiulo being beside him.

"You can call the five of us the barbershop quintet."

> —Crazy Joe Gallo hinting that he
> and four buddies had whacked
> Albert Anastasia at the Park
> Sheraton Hotel Barbershop.

"I am just a low uncouth person, I'm a low type sort of man. People of my caliber don't do nice things."

> —Willie Bioff testifying
> about his perjury.

"Ninety-nine times out of a hundred, a bomb like that should have killed him. Except, in the model of an Eldorado Cadillac, the manufacturer installed a steel floor plate beneath the driver's seat for added stability. It was the steel plate that saved Lefty's life. He should change his name from Lefty to Lucky."

> —Alcohol, Tobacco, and
> Firearms Agent John Rice.

"Johnny in a drum."

> —Wiseguys' lexicon of
> black humor to euphemize
> their grim trade.

"George, we hadda put a kimono on Bo."

> —Dutch Schultz's description of
> encasing Bo in a cement shroud and
> dropping him in the East River.

"You never get no back talk from no corpse."

> —Frank Capone, brother of Al.

"I got to give you credit, [assistant U.S. attorney Dan] Dorsky, you ended up getting me a life sentence with this Mickey Mouse case. Why don't you put me in the electric chair right here in the courtroom and get it over with now."

—Acting Colombo boss Andrew Russo after he was found guilty of obstruction of justice charges by the testimony of a former paramour who took up with a mob soldier.

"He's gonna get indicted any day, this moron. He's built himself a gallows. He's bought the noose. Look. You want a prediction? By June, her husband's gonna be indicted. And every two, three cents he's got, gonna be all tied up."

—John Gotti predicting that his daughter Victoria's husband, mob soldier Carmine Agnello, would be indicted by the feds.

"I don't know who shot me. It was somebody that didn't like me, I guess."

—Dutch Schultz.

"Maybe somebody somewhere down the line could tell me what the reason for this list is to begin with ... What do you need a list for? I don't understand that. Assume, uh, well, say you wanted to be a nice guy. Your wife was feeling under the weather, you wanted to go shopping, she gave you a list. After you bought your groceries, what do you do with the list, you put it away for posterity? To show that you went shopping one time?"

—John Gotti ridiculing his son
Junior for leaving lists of Mafia
members in a basement social
club where they were found and
seized by state investigators.

"How do I know? It's gotta be one of them coincidences."

—Marty Krompier, earner for Dutch
Schultz, on the connection between
being shot 100 minutes after Dutch.

"He's an imbecile. And you gotta see the charges. Malicious mopery. Possession of brains with intent to use. Malicious mopery. Malicious mopery. Stolen bumper. Hubcab."

—John Gotti complaining about his
mobster son-in-law Carmine
Agnello and the low-level charges
that have kept him from being
allowed to visit Gotti in prison.

"So what's the story with Carmine? Is he feeling good? Is he not feeling good? Is his medication increased? Decreased? Is it up? Down? Does he get in the back-seat of the car and think someone has stolen the steering wheel?"

> —John Gotti mocking his son-in-law's
> bouts with depression and other
> medical problems in a jailhouse
> visit with his daughter Victoria.

"You don't need to be ordering fancy duds. You're going to prison. Why don't you have a suit made with stripes on it?"

> —Frankie Rio to Al Capone who was
> at the tailor being measured for a suit.

"Not necessarily. When I went there they were out of red carpet."

> —Ralph "Bottles" Capone when asked
> by a special committee investigating
> organized crime whether they rolled the
> red carpet out for him at the dog races.

Wiseass Comments

 Frank & Fritzy on Squeaking

Frank: A squeaky wheel gets a little oil.

Fritzy: That's right, that's right.

Frank: If the wheel ain't squeaky it don't get nothin'.

Fritzy: That's right.

Frank: The squeaky wheel gets some oil.

Fritzy: That's right. That, you, you, you said it right. You said it right.

Women

"Listen to me. Don't let her go out with other women because women talk. And if she's with Anglo women they'll give her ideas and the next thing you know she'll want to go out more and more. Keep her at home because those women will put bad ideas in her head."

—Santo Trafficante's advice on
keeping his women home.

"They can't be everything, Che. You want a lover, a wife, a friend, a mother, a sister, a traveling companion, a business partner. It's too much."

—Santo Trafficante explaining how most
men expected too much of women.

"Johnny always had a girl on his arm. If there were ten girls at a table, Rosselli wanted all ten of them."

—Jimmy Starr, film columnist, reporting
on Rosselli's reputation with women.

"I've got a wonderful wife but everybody in Cuba has a mistress, even Batista. You've got to have fun in this world."

—Santo Trafficante.

"It's the same fucking story all the time. He's with a young broad, he's feeding her all kinds of money and jewelry and champagne, and everything, uh, that's why she's with him. Figures, look, what a score. I told Joey. 'You cocksucker. Why didn't you buy this (jewelry) for your daughter and your wife?'"

—DeCavalcante capo Vincent
"Vinny Ocean" Palermo voicing his
anger about the lowlife behavior
of associate Joseph Massella.

"Have you ever seen a gangster's moll? They have some pips. I got one in the car. Can I bring her in?"

—Hearse driver describing
a mourner who identified herself
as Mrs. Flegenheimer, Dutch
Schultz's wife number 3.

"That's a thing about wiseguys. You can go out and kill somebody, but don't swear in front of a female. And if a female swears, she's a *putana*—a whore."

—FBI agent Joe Pistone, noting that
that Benjamin "Lefty Guns" Ruggiero
said he would throw his wife Louise out
the window if she said the word *fuck*.

"When I walked into these places with Henry everyone came over. He introduced me to everyone. Everybody wanted to be nice to him. And he knew how to handle it all. It was so different from the other boys I went out with. They all seemed like kids. They used to take me to movies, bowling, the kinds of things you do when you're eighteen and your boyfriend is twenty-two."

—Karen Hill about the early days with Henry Hill.

"Six fucking weeks [Rusty's] got me out there [in Canada]. You're not allowed to make a phone call to your family. Good thing I had an ex-wife then who understood, never asked questions what happened to me or anything like that. Six fucking weeks. Now, I taught my new wife, Louise; 'Look, anything happens, you don't see me come in, don't you yell for anybody—he just didn't come home, you don't know nothing.' I says, 'You wanna cry, it's your fucking business. Don't ask anybody on the corner where I'm at or question my sister. Just say, 'He didn't come home—this is what my husband told me to say and these are his orders, and that's it.'"

—Lefty Guns Ruggiero.

Mob Molls: In or Out?

FBI agent William Roemer Jr.: Whoa, wait a minute here, Hump. That had nothing to do with families. That girl isn't family.

Chicago gangster Murray "Hump" Humphrey: You tell that to Frankie, Bill. And I agree with him, she's family.

Roemer: Hump, mistresses don't count. I had no idea you would include mistresses in your definition of "family."

Hump: Well, they should be. From now on, they count.

Roemer: I'll tell you what. I'll take it up with my guys and get back to you on it. But you know my feelings, mistresses don't count.

Hump: Bill, there may come a day, when you regret this. You might not always be so righteous.

"Once Karen threw away all their car keys and [Henry] got on a bike and had to peddle four miles to my place."

—Henry Hill's girlfriend Linda.

"The day before I went in [to prison] I took Linda to
the top of the Empire State Building. It was the first
time in my life I had ever gone up there. I told her that
I was going away in the morning .... I told her that if I
had half a million dollars I'd take her away with me to
Brazil in a minute, but I didn't have half a million, and,
anyway, I was a bum. I said that it was better if she
went her own way. I told her it was time for her to
move on. Don't waste any more time with me. It was
the end. I kissed her goodbye. We were both crying
and I watched her go down in the elevator."

—Henry Hill, describing his
breakup with his mistress.

"I know there are women who would have gotten out
of there the minute their boyfriend gave them a gun to
hide. 'A gun!' they would have yelled. 'Eek! Who needs
you? Get lost!' That's what a lot of girls, a lot of my
own girlfriends would have said the minute some guy
put a gun in their hands. But I've got to admit the
truth—it turned me on."

—Karen Hill.

"[Henry] came over to the side door. I could see he was
hurrying. He said, 'Hide it.' He had something cupped
in the palm of his hand. I took it and looked down. It
was a gun. It was small, heavy and gray. I couldn't
believe it. It felt so cold. It was a thrill just to hold it."

—Karen Hill.

"I'd have to say that Henry's friends were all very hard workers and hustlers …. Everybody worked somewhere. Nobody loafed. If anything, everyone was hustling all the time. I never saw people carrying guns. Later I found out that most of the time their wives were carrying them."

—Karen Hill.

"Friday was always the card-playing night. Later I found out that it was also the girlfriend night. Everybody who had a girlfriend took her out on Friday night. Nobody took his wife out on Friday night. The wives went out on Saturday night. That way there was no accident of running into somebody's wife when they were with their girlfriends."

—Karen Hill.

"[Henry] went to work every day. We all thought he was a bricklayer. He had a union card and everything. What did we know? It never occurred to me that it was strange that he had such nice smooth hands for a construction worker."

—Karen Hill describing her feelings about her "Wiseguy" husband Henry before she found out he was a drug dealer.

"When I was a child I would ask my grandma to tell my girlfriends about Al Capone, but instead of saying anything she would pull me into another room by my sleeve and say, 'Don't you tell those girls that we knew him.'"

—Grazia Antonucci's daughter.

"I don't know where he is. I don't know what he does. I am an old-fashioned woman. All I know is, he provides."

—Victoria Gotti to detectives who came to her door and asked her where her husband John was and what he did for a living.

"I was brought up to hold the door open for ladies."

—John Gotti as he held the courtroom door open for WCBS radio reporter Mary Gay Taylor with one hand and ushered her in with the other.

Frank & Fritzy on Current Events

Fritzy dozes off during the 10 o'clock news but Frankie quickly brings him up to speed and Fritzy is ready with a quick analysis.

Fritzy: What are you doing?

Frank: Watching Channel 5.

Fritzy: Yeah? I got the news on, I just dozed off.

Frank: About the gay community. About AIDS and everything.

Fritzy: Yeah?

Frank: Yeah.

Fritzy: Well, that's sad, really.

Frank: There's a woman here, she's married to a bisexual and she said she's happily married. She said she knows his lover and, uh, and the guy says to her, "Well, say if [UI] he was with a girl?" She says, "Then I would get mad."

Fritzy: In other words, but being he's with a guy she's not mad.

Frank: No.

Fritzy: Nice woman.

Your Point Is?

"There's creating, there's creating, and there's creating."
> —Frank Locascio trying
> to make a point.

"It's the chickens. The chickens. You can't get good chickens in Havana."
> —Lansky on one of the problems with
> Cuba during the Batista regime.

"You got all the kids coming around today, you know, and they're stronger than lions. And all these old guys, they got a brain of a seventy- or eighty-year-old person. A seventy-year-old brain can't compare with mine, because where he's got like twenty more years experience in his day, I got like fifty more years experience in my day. And we're living in my day, not their day anymore. That's what they fail to understand."
> —Dominick "Sonny Black"
> Napolitano trying to explain
> the Generation Gap.

"I'm Errol Flynn's younger brother."

> —A smiling Joe Bonanno, after hearing a teen-aged girl ask her friend if Bonanno, who was surrounded by photographers as he got off a plane after a long disappearance, were a movie star.

"That was the one thing about gangsters in those days, they wouldn't hold up people. They wouldn't rob a bank. If you got into their territory, you were in trouble, but the public didn't fear those people because they were never harmed."

> —Tony Berardi, newspaper photographer of Al Capone.

What'd They Say?

It's hard to believe that these two Luchese mob guys really knew what they were talking about.

Henry Bono: The friend of the girl's is going to speak to my friend tomorrow.

Frank Manzo: The water goes the other way [because] he no talk to me .... The boat turns the other way.

Bono: With you paddling or what.

Manzo: I give you plenty of rope, we catch the fish on the other side, ... the bait is in the water.

"Jeez, I'm sorry to hear that."

—Vincent "Chin" Gigante, after
hearing from John Gotti that his
son, Junior, had just been made.

"The only thing I know about organized crime is my
five ex-wives. Right now, I don't think I'm in danger
from anyone, except maybe the FBI."

—Morris Levy, former head of
Roulette Records, when questioned
about Chin Gigante and the
Genovese crime family.

"Bill, if anything ever happens to me, I hope you will
let those cocksuckers know that I was one of you, an
intelligence officer working undercover in the mob. I
want them to know that I doubled."

—Dick Cain, a made guy who
was an informer for FBI
Agent William Roemer Jr.

"I was just shooting at hawks."

—Genovese capo Anthony
"Tough Tony" Federici to cops who
arrested him for weapons possession
when they found him atop the roof
of his restaurant where he had come
to the aid of his racing pigeons.

"The hawks were murdering the defenseless pigeons for some time. They were flying away with them in their mouths, blood gushing from the hawks' mouths. For months this went on."

—Lawyer Mathew Mari explaining why Tough Tony Federici was permitted to dispose of weapons possession charges by paying a $90 fine.

"Hey kid, I'm no stranger. Your mother and father are from Ireland. My mother and father are from Ireland. I'm no stranger."

—Jimmy "Whitey" Bulger, South Boston hoodlum, to a young boy who refused ice cream from a "stranger."

 Frank & Fritzy: My Shrinking Mother-in-Law

Fritzy: Ya know what my wife told me?

Frank: Hah?

Fritzy: My wife told me about my mother-in-law. My mother-in-law hurt her vertebras goin' back. She broke her back. All, real tough time she had.

Frank: Yeah.

Fritzy: Do you know that woman shrunk three inches?

Frank: Uh-huh.

Fritzy: Because of the disintegrating vertebras?

Frank: Yeah.

Fritzy: Three inches!

Cast of Characters

Joseph "Joe Batters" Accardo   Long-time consigliere of the Chicago Outfit and one of the nation's most powerful Mafia leaders for more than 40 years till his death in 1992.

Blagio Adornetto   A one-time rising star in the John Stanfa–led Philadelphia Mafia who turned on Stanfa after Stanfa tried to have him whacked for making moves towards Stanfa's eldest daughter.

Carmine Agnello   A Gambino family soldier who married the boss's daughter, Victoria Gotti, but eventually fell out of favor with both his wife and his Mafia boss.

Joseph "Joey Doves" Aiuppa   Chicago Outfit boss whose reign ended after the FBI stumbled onto a vast Las Vegas skimming operation and expanded its investigation into a case that ultimately led to his arrest, indictment, and conviction on racketeering charges.

Gus Alex   A powerful, non-Italian Chicago Outfit associate who oversaw the corruption of politicians, judges, police, and union leaders until electronic surveillance and a turncoat ended his career.

Vinnie Aloi   A savvy Colombo family capo who was an acting boss of the family several times in the 1970s and 1980s and who tried to mediate a peace agreement during the bloody family war in the early 1990s.

Albert Anastasia   Feared Mafia boss whose brazen murder while having his hair cut in a Manhattan hotel barbershop still ranks among the Mafia's most infamous hits.

Anthony "Tough Tony" Anastasio   Long-time mob power on the Brooklyn docks whose strength faded after the killing of his brother Albert Anastasia in 1957.

Vincent "Jimmy" Angellino   A Colombo family capo who served as an acting family boss until the crime family decided to kill him.

Gennaro Angiulo   An egotistical New England Mafia underboss whose reign came to an inglorious end when the FBI bugged his Boston headquarters, leading to a 45-year prison term.

Grazia Antonucci   A pseudonym used by author Lawrence Bergreen to describe a woman member of a family who reputedly hid and befriended Al Capone in the mid 1920s and provided details about it decades later.

Salvatore "Sammy Meatballs" Aparo   A Genovese family capo who operated out of a Greenwich Village restaurant.

Vincent Aparo   Son of Sammy Meatballs and member of his father's mob crew.

Joe "Piney" Armone   A Gambino family drug dealer in the 1960s who was an underboss under John Gotti and who died in prison during Gotti's 1992 murder and racketeering trial.

Vincent Asaro   Bonanno capo convicted of lying on an application for a New York State driver's license and sentenced to four years in prison.

Beecher Avants   A Las Vegas homicide detective.

Cast of Characters

Salvatore Avellino A Luchese capo who controlled the private sanitation industry on Long Island and whose bugged car produced tapes used to help convict three New York mob bosses in the famous Mafia Commission case of 1986.

Salvatore Avena Lawyer son of a slain Philadelphia gangster whose bugged law office revealed his dispute with the Genovese family over garbage as well as details of an ongoing internal uprising against then–Philadelphia boss John Stanfa.

Anthony "Bowat" Baratta A Luchese capo convicted of racketeering and drug dealing.

Maria Barton An assistant U.S. Attorney who prosecuted wiseguys in Manhattan Federal Court.

Rosario Bellocchi A Sicilian-born favorite of beleaguered Philadelphia boss John Stanfa who won the heart of Stanfa's daughter but who eventually turned on his mentor from the witness stand.

Tony Berardi A Chicago newspaper photographer whose reminiscence of his encounters with Al Capone during Prohibition provided insight about the era and the notorious gangster.

Thomas Bilotti A key aide of Mafia boss Paul Castellano and a fellow murder victim in 1985.

Willie Bioff A Chicago Outfit associate who testified about the extortion of the nation's motion picture industry in the 1930s and paid for it by being blown to bits in 1955.

Robert "Bobby Cabert" Bisaccia A Gambino soldier who rose to capo after carrying out a mob hit for Mafia boss John Gotti.

Joseph Bonanno A New York Mafia boss who was deposed by the Mafia Commission and retired to Tucson, Arizona, where he authored a book about his life and enjoyed the fruits of his family's illegal activities.

Salvatore "Bill" Bonanno   Son of Joseph Bonanno who was inducted into his father's crime family and has made a cottage industry out of rewriting history to present his father and himself in a positive light as the most honorable of men.

Tore Bonanno   A grandson of infamous Mafioso Joseph Bonanno and son of gangster Salvatore "Bill" Bonanno.

Salvatore "Twitch" Brunetti   A John Stanfa associate whose claims to infamy were his hyperactivity and his many failed attempts to kill Stanfa rival Joey Merlino.

Angelo Bruno   A Philadelphia Mafia boss whose 1980 execution spawned two decades of violence under several successors, notably Nicodemo (Nicky) Scarfo.

James "Whitey" Bulger   Boston's most powerful and well-connected Irish gangster who became an FBI informant to undermine the New England Mafia and kill off his underworld rivals. He is on the FBI's Top Ten List of Most Wanted Fugitives.

Vincent "Fish" Cafaro   A Genovese soldier who changed his mind several times about becoming a cooperating witness but eventually did and testified against John Gotti and other top gangsters.

Louis Campagna   A onetime bodyguard for Al Capone, Campagna was one of several Chicago Outfit mobsters who were convicted in 1943 of an extortion scheme involving the motion picture industry. He died of natural causes in 1955.

Frank "Frank Campy" Campanella   A Colombo family associate who beat one racketeering case but didn't press his luck the second time he was indicted, accepting a plea bargain of less than four years in jail.

Al Capone   The transplanted Brooklyn gangster who took over the Chicago Outfit and became the most notorious gangster in America during the Prohibition era.

Cast of Characters

Frank Capone   The older brother of Al Capone who was killed in a 1924 shootout with Chicago cops during election day violence in the mob-controlled suburb of Cicero.

Ralph "Bottles" Capone   A brother of Al Capone and a low-level gangster who oversaw the Chicago Outfit's bottling plants during Prohibition.

Nicholas "The Crow" Caramandi   A capo who became a cooperating witness and wreaked havoc for Philadelphia mob boss Nicodemo "Little Nicky" Scarfo.

Anthony Cardinale   Noted Boston-based defense lawyer responsible for uncovering and exposing longtime corrupt activities by Boston FBI agents.

John Carneglia   A Gambino soldier and close friend of Mafia boss John Gotti.

John "Boobie" Cerasani   A powerful Bonanno soldier and close friend of the capo who unwittingly allowed an FBI agent to infiltrate the family.

Richard Chaisson   A buddy of New York mob associate Eddie Maloney.

James Chickara   A mob-connected New York businessman who dabbled in stock fraud and other schemes with the Colombo family.

Anthony "Sonny" Ciccone   A Gambino capo who ran the Brooklyn waterfront during John Gotti's reign.

Brenda and Philip Colletti   A pathetic street couple on the fringes of the Philadelphia mob who tried to improve their status and financial position by attempting to murder Joey Merlino, rival of boss John Stanfa.

Joseph Colombo   A celebrity Mafia boss who founded the Italian American Civil Rights League and picketed the FBI, claiming the agency was prejudiced against Italian Americans. He was shot at a League rally in 1971, lingering in a vegetative state until he died in 1978.

John Connolly   A well-connected Boston FBI agent who convinced James "Whitey" Bulger and Steve "The Rifleman" Flemmi to become FBI informants. He was highly praised for his role in the decimation of the Boston-area Mafia but was later exposed as corrupt and sentenced to 10 years in federal prison.

Joe Butch Corrao   A Little Italy–based Gambino capo and restaurateur who hosted many business dinners for John Gotti and company.

Paul Corsetti   A crime reporter for the *Boston Herald*.

Frank Costello   Politically well-connected New York Mafia boss who became a household name after his televised appearance before the Kefauver Hearings in the early 1950s.

Steven Crea   A labor racketeer who served as the Luchese family's representative at sit-downs to resolve construction industry disputes and also served for a time as the family's acting boss.

Frank Cullotta   A turncoat mob associate of Chicago/ Las Vegas hood Anthony Spilotro.

Bruce Cutler   Lawyer who won three straight cases representing John Gotti but was disqualified from representing him at the 1992 murder and racketeering trial in which Gotti was convicted and sentenced to life in prison.

Jack D'Amico   A Gambino capo who was a constant companion of John Gotti during his reign and was the Dapper Don's biggest cheerleader at his 1992 racketeering and murder trial.

Cast of Characters

J. Richard Davis   A lawyer for infamous Prohibition era mobster Dutch Schultz who was most responsible for creating a myth that scores of old-fashioned "Moustache Pete" Mafia bosses were massacred after the 1931 murder of top boss Salvatore Maranzano.

Pam Davis   An assistant U.S. Attorney in Brooklyn in the Organized Crime and Racketeering section.

Raymond Dearie   A former U.S. Attorney who presided over many organized crime trials as a Federal Court judge in Brooklyn.

Frank DeCicco   Key member of John Gotti's plot to kill Mafia boss Paul Castellano who paid for his participation by being blown to bits by a bomb that was placed under his car and detonated by remote control.

Michael "Iron Mike" DeFeo   A federal prosecutor with the Justice Department's Organized Crime Strike Force.

Thomas "Tommy" DelGiorno   A Philadelphia capo for Nicky Scarfo who turned on the mob when the feds told him that he was in trouble with his old gangster buddies.

Aniello Dellacroce   A longtime underboss to Carlo Gambino who remained the family's number two man under Paul Castellano, Dellacroce was a mentor and advisor to John Gotti.

Sam "Mad Sam" DeStefano   An aging, violent, erratic Chicago Outfit soldier whose declining mental health and mounting legal problems resulted in his shotgun murder in his own garage.

Thomas DiBella   An aged Colombo capo selected by imprisoned boss Carmine "Junior" Persico in the mid 1970s to be a caretaker boss until Persico could win his own release.

Thomas DiFiore A Long Island–based Bonanno capo who gravitated into the lucrative adult porn industry.

Bastiano "Buster" Domingo A murderous New York gangster from the Prohibition era whose exploits became known during the 1963 revelations of turncoat mobster Joseph Valachi.

Murray Ehrenberg Manager of the Stardust Casino during the Frank "Lefty" Rosenthal era.

James "Jimmy Brown" Failla Bodyguard/chauffeur for Carlo Gambino who moved up to capo and supervised the crime family's rackets in the private sanitation industry for decades under Gambino, Paul Castellano, and John Gotti.

Frank "The Beast" Falanga A Colombo family associate and loan shark who was convicted along with the family's leadership in 1986 and dropped dead the following day.

Anthony "Tough Tony" Federici A Queens-based Genovese capo with a soft spot in his heart for racing pigeons.

Frank "Frankie Pearl" Federico A Luchese soldier who was nabbed for murder in a Bronx coffee shop after 10 years as one of America's most-wanted fugitives.

Bob Fitzpatrick A Boston-based FBI agent who was suspicious of the relationship that gangster Whitey Bulger had with other FBI agents.

Steve "The Rifleman" Flemmi A longtime mob associate from Boston who threw in with the leader of the Irish gang and became an FBI informer to bring down his mob cronies while enriching himself.

Johnny Formosa A Las Vegas–based gopher for Chicago boss Sam "Momo" Giancana who was tape recorded urging Giancana to lean on singer Frank Sinatra to use his connections to the Kennedy family to ease the FBI pressure on Giancana.

Cast of Characters

Jim Fox New York FBI boss during the investigation and successful 1992 prosecution of swashbuckling New York Mafia boss John Gotti.

Tony Francesehi A New York mob wannabe loosely connected by marriage to the Luchese family.

Cammy Franzese Second wife of turncoat Colombo capo Michael "The Yuppie Don" Franzese who was instrumental in converting the mobster into a born-again Christian.

John "Sonny" Franzese Father of Michael and a legendary Colombo gangster who just keeps on trucking. He was incarcerated for his fourth federal parole violation at age 85 and is due to be released from prison in 2004 shortly before his eighty-seventh birthday.

Michael "The Yuppie Don" Franzese A Colombo capo who made millions of dollars in the bootleg gasoline business and then turned on the mob when he was indicted. He lived to write about his life in a best selling book.

Aladena "Jimmy the Weasel" Fratianno The second "made man" to break the Mafia's vow of silence and testify against the mob.

Anthony "Nino" Gaggi A Gambino capo who said he wanted to die on the streets of New York with a gun in his hand but dropped dead of a heart attack in a federal prison in Manhattan.

Crazy Joe Gallo A notorious New York mobster who befriended celebrities and was shot to death in a landmark Little Italy clam house.

James Gallo DeCavalcante soldier nabbed in a mob hit the New Jersey–based crime family committed as a favor to Gambino boss John Gotti.

Carlo Gambino An illegal immigrant who became one of the most powerful Mafia bosses in American history, dying of natural causes in 1976.

Tommy Gambino Son of the crime family patriarch, Gambino was a college-educated, multimillionaire Garment Center businessman who threw in with John Gotti after he took over the crime family by killing Gambino's uncle, Paul Castellano.

Vito Genovese A powerful New York gangster who died in federal prison while serving time for dealing in drugs.

Sam "Momo" Giancana A Chicago Outfit boss—made famous by his violent reactions to relentless FBI pressure and his consorting with celebrities—who was shot to death by his peers in 1975.

Rev. Louis Gigante Chief spokesman for his brother, Mafia boss Vincent "Chin" Gigante, and a longtime leading advocate for the proposition that Vincent was a mentally ill former boxer and not a cunning Mafia boss.

Vincent "Chin" Gigante Cunning Mafia boss who avoided prosecution for three decades by feigning insanity as he stumbled around Greenwich Village in his pajamas but was convicted of racketeering in 1997 and admitted in 2003 that he had fooled doctors for years about his mental health.

Frank Gioia Jr. A Luchese soldier who decided to cooperate with the feds when he learned that his crime family had marked his father for death.

Allen Glick An ambitious mob-connected Las Vegas entrepreneur whose casino empire was funded by the Mafia-controlled Teamsters Central States Pension Fund.

Cast of Characters

John Gotti The swashbuckling Dapper Don who burst on the scene after the midtown Manhattan assassination of Mafia boss Paul Castellano, and died of cancer in a federal prison hospital while serving a life sentence for five murders, including Castellano's.

John A. "Junior" Gotti The Junior Don who followed his father into the mob and then into federal prison when he pleaded guilty to racketeering. He was sentenced to 77 months—a term that ends in September 2004.

Peter Gotti The older brother of the Dapper Don who took over the crime family and followed his brother into federal prison.

Salvatore "Wayne" Grande A Philadelphia wiseguy whose chief claim to fame was his 1984 "ambush" murder of capo Salvatore "Salvie" Testa, son of a slain Philadelphia boss.

Salvatore "Sammy Bull" Gravano A superstar prosecution witness when he emerged as the first mob underboss to testify against his Mafia boss, he received a controversial five-year sentence for a life of crime that included 19 murders and was later nabbed for dealing drugs with his wife, son, and daughter and sentenced to 20 years in prison.

Michael "Mikey Gal" Guerrieri A Gambino soldier and longtime buddy of John Gotti.

Henry Hill Coke-snorting mob associate who cooperated against Luchese capo Paul Vario and Jimmy "The Gent" Burke, the murderous mastermind of the $5.8 million robbery of Lufthansa Airlines that was the focal point of *Wiseguy*, the Nicholas Pileggi book that was adapted for the big screen as *Goodfellas*, starring Ray Liotta as Hill and Robert De Niro as the Jimmy Burke character.

Karen Hill   A naive young Jewish woman—played by Lorraine Bracco in *Goodfellas*, the movie about Hill's life— whose attraction to Henry Hill and his gangster life led to decades of tumultuous marriage, drug use, fear, and ultimately divorce.

James R. "Jimmy" Hoffa   Mob-connected Teamsters Union president who was killed in 1975 when he bucked his former mob friends.

J. Edgar Hoover   The controversial FBI director who ordered agents to buttress traditional investigative techniques with extensive illegal electronic surveillance, dubious informant programs, and media leaks to enable the agency to get up to speed on Mafia activities after he was embarrassed by the FBI's lack of information about the mob in the late 1950s.

Murray "Hump" Humphrey   A longtime Chicago Outfit power, despite his Welsh background, who led many successful Outfit efforts to corrupt law enforcement and other public officials who threatened to harm their rackets.

Joseph Ida   A Genovese soldier who raced pigeons in his down time.

Lawrence "Fat Larry" Iorizzo   A Colombo family associate who was the point man in the crime family's lucrative bootleg gasoline rackets until he was nailed by the feds and decided to cooperate against his former friends.

Joey the Hitman   A pseudonym for an alleged mob hitman who matter-of-factly described a life of crime that included 38 victims in a sometimes hard-to-believe book that made *The New York Times* best seller list.

Jimmy Katz and Chico Krantz   Two low-level Boston hoodlums targeted as possible cooperating witnesses by federal prosecutors looking to make a case against notorious South Side gangster Whitey Bulger.

Cast of Characters

Marty Krompier   A close associate and big earner for Dutch Schultz during the Prohibition era.

June Lang   A 1930s-era Hollywood supporting actress who was briefly married to Chicago hood Johnny Rosselli in the early 1940s.

Philip Leonetti   Philadelphia underboss and nephew to Nicodemo Scarfo who turned on his uncle and the crime family and cut his prison time from 45 years to less than 6.

Dennis Lepore   An enforcer for the New England Mafia.

Barry Levin   Longtime lawyer for Colombo family gangster Alphonse Persico.

Peter Limone   A veteran Boston mobster who spent 33 years in prison after being falsely convicted of murder based on the perjured testimony of a witness that the FBI allegedly knew had testified falsely at the time of his trial.

Frank Lino   A Bonanno capo who became a cooperating witness for the feds in 2003.

Charles "Lucky" Luciano   Mob boss credited with creating a "Mafia Commission" of bosses to set policy and settle disputes among crime families. Often called Charlie Lucky, his given name was Salvatore Lucania. Jailed for organizing a prostitution ring, he was deported to Italy and died in 1962.

Stefano Magaddino   A longtime Buffalo Mafia boss and influential member of the Mafia Commission for more than 30 years.

Eddie Maloney   A New York mob associate who kidnapped wiseguys and lived to tell about it.

Venero "Benny Eggs" Mangano   A Garment Center businessman who doubled as the Genovese family underboss, and refused to testify against his boss.

Salvatore Maranzano   Powerful New York–based Mafia leader during the Prohibition era who briefly rose to the top of the Mafia heap in 1931 only to be murdered in the same year by rivals led by Charles "Lucky" Luciano.

Carlos Marcello   Powerful New Orleans Mafia boss who was a prime target of Robert Kennedy and who die-hard conspiracy theorists still link to the assassination of President John Kennedy.

Mathew Mari   New York lawyer who represented the first mobster to be prosecuted under revised federal death penalty statutes.

Tommy Marrone   An enforcer for the Philadelphia Mafia family.

Fred Martens   Executive director of the Pennsylvania Crime Commission.

Joseph Massino   A cagey, surveillance-conscious Bonanno family soldier who took over the crime family in 1991, escaping the long clutches of the law until 2003, when he was hit with racketeering and murder charges.

Charles B. McLaughlin   District attorney of the Bronx during the Prohibition era.

James Messera   Genovese capo and convicted labor racketeer.

Liborio "Louie" Milito   Gambino soldier killed by John Gotti and Sammy Bull Gravano.

Lynda Milito   Wife of Louie Milito and author.

Anthony Mirra   A Bonanno soldier deeply involved in heroin trafficking who was shot to death in 1982 after falling out of favor with the family.

Cast of Characters

Evelyn Mittelman   Girlfriend of 1940s-era gangster Harry Strauss who was also known as Pittsburgh Phil.

Ronald "Messy Marvin" Moran   A young associate of the Colombo and Luchese families who decided to cooperate when the feds nailed him on racketeering charges.

Dominick "Sonny Black" Napolitano   A Bonanno capo who paid with his life in 1981 for letting FBI agent Joe "Donnie Brasco" Pistone infiltrate the crime family.

Ralph Natale   A longtime mob associate who was inducted and made front boss of the Philadelphia family after completing a long stretch in prison. A few years later he became the first Mafia boss to testify against his "friends" when faced with another lengthy prison sentence.

Warren Olney III   A California attorney general.

Victor "Little Vic" Orena   A onetime Colombo family acting boss who headed a rebel faction that waged a bloody mob war in a vain effort to win control of the crime family.

Vincent "Vinny Ocean" Palermo   A capo on a DeCavalcante family ruling panel who cooperated with the feds after his 1999 indictment for racketeering and murder.

Joe Paterno   A Gambino capo whose chief notoriety came when his scheme to have a relative murdered for her money was featured on a national television news show.

Alphonse Persico   A college-educated gangster who followed his father into the Colombo crime family and made it to acting boss.

Carmine "Junior" Persico   A jailed-for-life Mafia boss who selected his son Alphonse to carry out his legacy atop the Colombo mob.

Frank Persico   A Colombo family associate who ran a stable of corrupt stockbrokers while serving as the crime family's man on Wall Street.

Anthony Piccolo   A veteran Philadelphia mobster who had the misfortune of being the family consigliere during the revolt-plagued regime of boss John Stanfa in the early 1990s.

Louis Pichini   An assistant U.S. Attorney who led the prosecution team in the 1988 racketeering trial in which Philadelphia boss Nicky Scarfo and 16 underlings were convicted and received lengthy prison sentences.

Joe "Donnie Brasco" Pistone   An FBI agent played by Johnny Depp in the movie *Donnie Brasco* who posed as wannabe gangster Donnie Brasco as he infiltrated the Bonanno crime family in the late 1970s.

Ruth Pollack   Award-winning New York courtroom sketch artist.

John Pollok   An attorney whose name was occasionally uttered—and sometimes forgotten—by John Gotti during his rants against the high cost of legal fees.

Sam Pontarelli   Sam Pontarelli, a pseudonym created by author Lawrence Bergreen for a Chicago native who spent some time as a young man at Chicago Cubs baseball games in the company of Al Capone and who also claimed that Eliot Ness had taken bribes from Capone's organization.

Salvatore Profaci   Son of late Colombo family boss Joseph Profaci and a New Jersey–based capo whose efforts to help a Philadelphia area relative in a dispute with the Genovese family—and many other mobster musings—were caught on tape by the FBI.

Cast of Characters

Frank Ragano   A disgraced, longtime lawyer for Tampa Mafia boss Santo Trafficante who later claimed in a book that the Mafia was involved in the assassination of President John F. Kennedy.

Abe "Kid Twist" Reles   An old-time gangster who fell to his death from the fifth floor of a Coney Island hotel after becoming a prosecution witness.

Frankie Rio   A Chicago gangster credited with saving Al Capone's life during a furious machine gun battle in a 1926 ambush by Capone rivals at the Hawthorne Inn in Cicero, Illinois.

William Roemer   A Chicago FBI agent who investigated the Mafia after FBI Director J. Edgar Hoover instituted the Top Hoodlum informant program in the late 1950s.

Louis Romano   A murderous Chicago gangster.

Frank "Lefty" Rosenthal   The Chicago Outfit's overseer of the Allen Glick group of skimmed Las Vegas casinos whose life was portrayed by Robert De Niro in *Casino*.

Geri Rosenthal   The beautiful, doomed, alcoholic wife of Las Vegas mogul Frank Rosenthal, portrayed by Sharon Stone in the movie *Casino*.

Johnny Rosselli   A Chicago gangster who made it big in Hollywood and Las Vegas.

Arnold "The Brain" Rothstein   A politically connected New York bookmaker and bootlegger, said by some to have been behind the fixing of the 1919 World Series, he was gunned down and killed over a gambling debt in 1928.

Angelo Ruggiero   A Gambino soldier and longtime friend of Mafia bosses John Gotti and Joseph Massino.

Benjamin "Lefty Guns" Ruggiero   A Bonanno soldier—played by Al Pacino in the movie *Donnie Brasco*—who became friendly with undercover FBI agent Joe Pistone and was convicted for racketeering and sentenced to 15 years in prison.

Andrew Russo   A Colombo capo and cousin of boss Carmine "Junior" Persico, who once served as the family's acting boss.

Frank Salemme   New England Mafia boss hit with racketeering charges along with longtime FBI informers Whitey Bulger and Steve "The Rifleman" Flemmi in the case that led to disclosures of decades of corrupt activities by Boston-based FBI agents.

Anthony "Fat Tony" Salerno   A onetime consigliere and acting boss of the Genovese crime family who died in federal prison serving a 100-year sentence for his racketeering conviction in the Mafia Commission case.

Steve Salvo   A linguistic expert used by the FBI to make sense of conversations among Sicilian-based drug dealers.

Joseph Santaguida   Philadelphia lawyer who represented many Philadelphia-based members of organized crime.

Gaetano "Tommy Horsehead" Scafidi   A not-too-swift Philadelphia wiseguy who was smart enough to cooperate with the feds to cut down on his time in federal prison.

Richard "Dick Cain" Scalzetti   A well-connected Chicago Outfit soldier who infiltrated area law enforcement in the early sixties and who later became a top-level FBI informant until he was killed in a dispute with another mobster.

Nicodemo "Little Nicky" Scarfo   Murderous, paranoid Philadelphia Mafia boss who ended up being sentenced to 69 years in federal prison.

Cast of Characters

Gregory Scarpa   A Colombo capo who was a leading killer in two family mob wars while serving at the same time as a top-echelon FBI informant for more than 30 years.

Leslie Scherr and Jacques Schiffer   Washington attorneys who represented Chicago hood Johnny Rosselli before a U.S. Senate Committee in the mid-1970s.

Edwin Schulman   An attorney who represented a few of John Gotti's friends.

Dutch Schultz   Legendary New York gangster who was killed in 1935 when the mob learned he intended to kill mob prosecutor Thomas Dewey.

Joseph Scopo   A Colombo capo and a major force in the rebel faction headed by Little Vic Orena until Persico loyalists ambushed and killed him in front of his Queens home.

Christopher Sexton   A prison guard who questioned Mafia boss Vincent Gigante about his prison accommodations.

Gerald Shargel   An attorney who represented John Gotti and some of his friends.

John "Red" Shea   A South Boston gangster under Whitey Bulger.

Benjamin "Bugsy" Siegel   A vicious Prohibition Era hood who gravitated to Las Vegas, Siegel had a tumultuous love affair with a beautiful gangster moll, Virginia Hill, that ended in spectacular fashion when he was shot to death in Hollywood in 1947.

Joe Sodano   A Philadelphia capo who controlled the family's North Jersey gambling and loan-sharking operations until his murder in 1995.

Salvatore "Shotsie" Sparacio   A longtime South Jersey bookmaker for the Philadelphia mob until he was convicted of racketeering in 1995 and sentenced to 30 years.

Anthony "The Ant" Spilotro   Vicious Chicago enforcer sent to Las Vegas as the muscle behind the Outfit's casino-skimming operations and ended up being buried alive when his bosses no longer trusted him.

John Stanfa   Sicilian-born hood whose surprising rise to the top of the Philadelphia family in the early 1990s was cut short by a racketeering and murder conviction and a life sentence in 1996.

Theresa Stanley   Longtime girlfriend of notorious Boston gangster Whitey Bulger who claimed to know nothing of his affairs—including a 20-years-long one with a younger woman for whom he dumped Stanley when he skipped out on a murder and racketeering indictment—when she was questioned by the feds.

Jimmy Starr   A Hollywood gossip columnist and casual friend of Johnny Rosselli.

Joseph "Hoboken Joe" Stassi   A veteran New Jersey–based Genovese family soldier.

Phil Steinberg   A cofounder of the highly successful Buddha record label in the 1960s who claimed he paid nothing to notorious Colombo mobster John "Sonny" Franzese to protect his company from extortion by other mobsters, a claim few take seriously.

Zachary "Red" Strate   A mob-connected Las Vegas developer.

Anthony "Tony Bender" Strollo   A longtime capo who enjoyed a brief burst of mob glory as acting boss for Vito Genovese when he was jailed for heroin dealing, Strollo quickly fell out of favor with Genovese and disappeared on April 8, 1962.

Cast of Characters

Anthony Stropoli   A previously unscathed Colombo soldier nabbed for three different crimes in less than nine months during a run of bad luck around the turn of the twenty-first century.

Salvatore "Salvie" Testa   A wiseguy whose father was the only Philadelphia Mafia boss to be blown up by rivals, Testa killed one of the assassins in 1982 on the anniversary of the bombing and stuffed firecrackers into the victim's mouth. Testa was killed two years later.

John A. Toomey   A Jesuit priest who spoke about the death of Dutch Schultz.

Ann Torrio   Wife of early Prohibition-era Chicago leader Johnny Torrio who saw him survive a murder attempt and lived to see him die of natural causes many years later.

Carmen Tortora   One of four inductees into the New England Mafia who was "made" during a ceremony that was tape recorded by the FBI.

Santo Trafficante   Tampa Mafia boss who controlled casinos in Cuba before Fidel Castro came into power.

James Traficant   A mob-connected Ohio congressman convicted of racketeering.

Dominick "Big Trin" Trinchera   A corpulent Bonanno capo who picked the wrong side in a crime family feud in 1981 and ended up in many pieces.

Joseph Valachi   A Genovese gangster who became the first American mobster to break the Mafia vow of *omerta* ("silence") and testify against the mob.

George Jay Vandermark   A Las Vegas gambler who devised the scheme to help the mob skim the Allen Glick casinos by rigging the scales to underweigh the coins.

Gaetano "Corky" Vastola A savvy DeCavalcante soldier who figured out how to infiltrate the music industry and how to evade a gaggle of gangsters who had marked him for death for a variety of reasons during the 1980s and 1990s.

John Veasey Tough Philadelphia mob hitman who turned on his wiseguy friends when the going got tough for him.

Rocco Vitulli A Luchese family gangster.

Tom Wadden A Washington attorney who helped represent Chicago mobster Johnny Rosselli before a U.S. Senate committee investigating links between the CIA and political assassinations.

Henry Whitaker A defense lawyer who handled cases with mob lawyer Frank Ragano.

Walter Winchell A legendary, powerful, well-connected newspaper columnist and radio commentator who often wrote about the comings and goings of big-time New York gangsters.

Larry Zannino A vicious, Boston-based New England capo who ended his life behind bars after being secretly taped by the FBI extolling the virtues of La Cosa Nostra.

George "Georgie Neck" Zappola A Luchese family capo well-versed in the art of killing.

Joseph "Bayonne Joe" Zicarelli A Newark-based mobster and close confidante of boss Simone "Sam the Plumber" DeCavalcante during his heyday in the 1960s.

Index

Index

Index

H–I

Hill, Henry, 4, 12, 137-138, 145, 149, 152, 157, 163, 180, 192, 196-197, 205, 216, 232-234

Hill, Karen, 115-116, 181, 232-235

Hill, Ralph, 59

Hines, Jimmy, 172

Hoffa, Jimmy, 1, 7, 37, 76, 81, 83, 95, 97, 109, 143, 149, 153, 170, 180, 203-204

Hoover, J. Edgar, 19, 94, 133

Hubbard, Lester T., 90

Humphrey, Murray "Hump," 84, 94, 133, 166, 218, 233

Ida, Joseph, 103

Iorizzo, Lawrence "Fat Larry," 132, 158

J–K

Johnson, Lyndon, 170

Katz, Jimmy, 93

Kelly, Stephen, 147

Kennedy, John, 19, 170-171

Kennedy, Joseph, 170

Kennedy, Robert, 19, 65, 91, 170

Khashoggi, Adnan, 131

Kline, Carl, 86

Kloud, Suzanne, 112

Krantz, Chico, 93

Krieger, Albert, 9, 37, 135

Krompier, Marty, 227

L

La Guardia, Fiorello, 90

LaMonte, John, 221

Lang, June, 113

Lansky, Meyer "Buddy," 45, 53, 68, 114, 125-126, 162, 164, 194, 199, 212, 219, 238

Lanza, Joe "Socks," 119

Leonetti, Philip, 10, 21, 139

Lepore, Dennis, 214

Levy, Morris, 45, 158, 240

Liberace, 7

Limone, Peter, 30

Lino, Edward, 50

Lister, Walter, 130

Locascio, Peter, 26, 72-73, 99-100, 238

Lonardo, Angelo, 188

Luciano, Lucky, 14, 40, 119, 129

Lynch, Ted, 87

M

Maas, Peter, 204

Madden, John, 106

Index

T–U

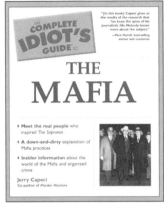
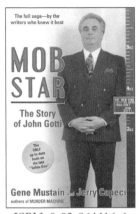